177246

LEARNING MACHINES

Foundations of trainable pattern-classifying systems

McGraw-Hill Series in Systems Science

EDITORIAL CONSULTANTS

George Dantzig
V. A. Balakrishnan
Lotfi Zadeh

Harrison, *Introduction to Switching and Automata Theory*
Nilsson, *Learning Machines: Foundations of Trainable Pattern-classifying Systems*
Papoulis, *Probability, Random Variables, and Stochastic Processes*
Zadeh and Desoer, *Linear System Theory: The State Space Approach*

LEARNING MACHINES

Foundations of trainable pattern-classifying systems

NILS J. NILSSON

Stanford Research Institute
Menlo Park, California

New York   St. Louis   San Francisco
Toronto   London   Sydney

McGRAW-HILL BOOK COMPANY

Learning Machines

Copyright © 1965 by McGraw-Hill, Inc.
All rights reserved. Printed in the
United States of America. This book,
or parts thereof, may not be reproduced
in any form without permission of the publishers.

Library of Congress Catalog Card Number: 64-8621

4 5 6 7 8 9 – M P – 9

46570

TO KAREN

PREFACE

This monograph presents some of the results of research in the new and exciting field of *learning machines*. A learning machine, broadly defined, is any device whose actions are influenced by past experiences. The present work deals specifically with the theory of a subclass of learning machines, those which can be *trained* to recognize patterns. Some well-known examples of trainable pattern-classifying systems are the PERCEPTRON and the MADALINE and MINOS networks.

The subject of trainable pattern-classifying machines is one aspect of artificial intelligence research about which a growing body of empirical and theoretical knowledge is beginning to emerge. It is the author's belief that the scope and depth of the developing theory is not yet generally appreciated by many researchers in the computer-related fields. Contributions to this theory have come from many disciplines including statistics, switching theory, physiological psychology, and automatic control theory. This monograph is an attempt to organize some of these results into a coherent, logical framework useful to students and researchers alike.

The basic approach adopted in this book involves the concept of *discriminant functions* that define the behavior of the pattern-classifying machine. A trainable pattern-classifying machine is then defined as one with "adjustable" discriminant functions. Within the framework provided by this approach, most of the previous and present work in the field is interpreted as attempts either to understand the properties of various discriminant functions or to find methods for their selection or adjustment.

The following topics are given special treatment:

1. Parametric and nonparametric training methods. The decision-theoretic approach is an example of the former, while the iterative weight-adjustment (or "adaptive") approach is an example of the latter.

2. Properties of various families of discriminant functions used by trainable machines.

3. Training theorems (including proofs of the perceptron convergence theorem).

4. Training methods for networks of threshold logic units.

The level of exposition assumes that the reader is familiar with elementary probability theory and simple matrix manipulations. Many of the arguments presented appeal to geometric intuition.

Collecting the significant results in a new and growing field is a risky venture. The probability of having overlooked some worthy material in the preparation of this monograph is high. An example of a deliberate omission is the subject of measurement selection, sometimes called preprocessing. The selection of the measurements or properties on which recognition is based is one of the most important problems in pattern recognition. Yet while there have been many schemes advanced for *testing* the worth of already selected measurements, the author is not aware of any general methods for directing an efficient *search* for useful measurements. Perhaps the next few years will see progress on this vital problem. Other subjects related to those discussed in this book but not included because they are well treated elsewhere are stochastic approximation and iterative gradient techniques.

This monograph had its origins in courses taught by the author in the Electrical Enginering Departments of Stanford University and the University of California, Berkeley, in 1962 and 1964, respectively. Professors N. Abramson and T. Cover of Stanford and L. Zadeh of the University of California gave many helpful suggestions for improving the book. Discussions with Dr. Louis Fein, Consultant, helped to clarify some fundamental concepts.

The author would like to express his gratitude to the Stanford Research Institute for its support and encouragement in this project. Thanks are due to Dr. C. A. Rosen of SRI, whose enthusiasm originally interested the author in this subject and who has provided valued support and direction. Various agencies of the U.S. Government, including the Office of Naval Research, the Rome Air Development Center, and the U.S. Army Electronics Research and Development Laboratories have sponsored learning-machine research at SRI, and it is this sponsorship which has made it possible for the author to work in this field.

It is impossible to acknowledge all of the important influences on the author's views of this field. He has benefited materially from continuing discussions with colleagues associated with the Learning Machines Group of SRI. The author is particularly grateful to Dr. Richard Duda for his thoughtful and detailed criticism of the entire manuscript; his suggestions substantially improved the readability and rigor of the presentation.

NILS J. NILSSON

CONTENTS

Preface, vii

1 TRAINABLE PATTERN CLASSIFIERS — 1

1.1 Machine classification of data, 1
1.2 The basic model, 2
1.3 The problem of what to measure, 4
1.4 Decision surfaces in pattern space, 4
1.5 Discriminant functions, 6
1.6 The selection of discriminant functions, 8
1.7 Training methods, 9
1.8 Summary of book by chapters, 11
1.9 Bibliographical and historical remarks, 12
References, 12

2 SOME IMPORTANT DISCRIMINANT FUNCTIONS: THEIR PROPERTIES AND THEIR IMPLEMENTATIONS — 15

2.1 Families of discriminant functions, 15
2.2 Linear discriminant functions, 16
2.3 Minimum-distance classifiers, 16
2.4 The decision surfaces of linear machines, 18
2.5 Linear classifications of patterns, 20
2.6 The threshold logic unit (TLU), 21
2.7 Piecewise linear discriminant functions, 24
2.8 Quadric discriminant functions, 27
2.9 Quadric decision surfaces, 28
2.10 Implementation of quadric discriminant functions, 28
2.11 Φ functions, 30
2.12 The utility of Φ functions for classifying patterns, 31
2.13 The number of linear dichotomies of N points of d dimensions, 32

CONTENTS

2.14 The effects of constraints, 35
2.15 The number of Φ function dichotomies, 37
2.16 Machine capacity, 38
2.17 Bibliographical and historical remarks, 40
References, 41

3 PARAMETRIC TRAINING METHODS 43

3.1 Probabilistic pattern sets, 43
3.2 Discriminant functions based on decision theory, 44
3.3 Likelihoods, 45
3.4 A special loss function, 46
3.5 An example, 47
3.6 The bivariate normal probability-density function, 50
3.7 The multivariate normal distribution, 54
3.8 The optimum classifier for normal patterns, 55
3.9 Some special cases involving identical covariance matrices, 56
3.10 Training with normal pattern sets, 57
3.11 Learning the mean vector of normal patterns, 58
3.12 Bibliographical and historical remarks, 61
References, 62

4 SOME NONPARAMETRIC TRAINING METHODS FOR Φ MACHINES 65

4.1 Nonparametric training of a TLU, 65
4.2 Weight space, 66
4.3 TLU training procedures, 69
4.4 A numerical example of error-correction training, 72
4.5 An error-correction training procedure for $R > 2$, 75
4.6 Applications to Φ machines, 76
4.7 Bibliographical and historical remarks, 76
References, 77

5 TRAINING THEOREMS 79

5.1 The fundamental training theorem, 79
5.2 Notation, 81
5.3 Proof 1, 82
5.4 Proof 2, 85

5.5 A training theorem for R-category linear machines, 87
5.6 A related training theorem for the case $R = 2$, 90
5.7 Bibliographical and historical remarks, 92
References, 93

6 LAYERED MACHINES 95

6.1 Layered networks of TLUs, 95
6.2 Committee machines, 97
6.3 A training procedure for committee machines, 99
6.4 An example, 101
6.5 Transformation properties of layered machines, 103
6.6 A sufficient condition for image-space linear separability, 107
6.7 Derivation of a discriminant function for a layered machine, 109
6.8 Bibliographical and historical remarks, 113
References, 113

7 PIECEWISE LINEAR MACHINES 115

7.1 Multimodal pattern-classifying tasks, 115
7.2 Training PWL machines, 116
7.3 A disadvantage of the error-correction training methods, 118
7.4 A nonparametric decision procedure, 119
7.5 Nonparametric decisions based on distances to modes, 121
7.6 Mode-seeking and related training methods for PWL machines, 122
7.7 Bibliographical and historical remarks, 125
References, 126

APPENDIX 127

A.1 Separation of a quadratic form into positive and negative parts, 127
A.2 Implementation, 128
A.3 Transformation of normal patterns, 131

INDEX 133

LEARNING MACHINES

Foundations of trainable pattern-classifying systems

CHAPTER 1

TRAINABLE PATTERN CLASSIFIERS

1·1 Machine classification of data

At the forefront of research supporting the current technological revolution lies the challenging prospect of mechanizing a wide variety of intellectual tasks which heretofore have been performed only by humans. Already, for example, there have been some moderately successful attempts to endow machines with the ability to play chess, predict the weather, prove theorems, recognize speech sounds, diagnose diseases, sort photographs, and read handwriting.

Many of these tasks involve the ability to classify or sort data. One example of a sorting task is weather prediction. A forecast must be based on certain weather measurements, for example, the present values of atmospheric pressure and atmospheric pressure changes at a number of stations. Suppose that today the forecaster wishes to predict whether or not it will rain tomorrow at a certain station. In effect he must be able to sort or place a given set of measured weather data into one of two categories: (a) those data that indicate rain tomorrow, and (b) those data that

2   TRAINABLE PATTERN CLASSIFIERS

do not. To be successful the classification must be performed in such a way that the resulting forecast and the actual outcome are, on the average, in close agreement.

Other data-sorting tasks include speech and character recognition, medical diagnosis, and speaker identification. The mechanization of any of these jobs requires a device which accepts input data and responds with an output indicating the classification of this data. Table 1·1 shows several sorting tasks and the appropriate inputs and responses of the classifier.

TABLE 1·1   A list of sorting tasks

Task	Input data	Response
Weather prediction	Weather measurements	Forecast
Handwritten-character recognition	Optical signal	Name of character
Medical diagnosis	Symptoms	Name of disease
Speech recognition	Acoustic waveform	Name of word
Speaker recognition	Acoustic waveform	Name of speaker
Photographic sorting	Optical signal	Category of photograph

The purpose of this book is to present a unified treatment of the mathematical theory underlying the design of data-classifying machines. Some aspects of this general theory derive from a branch of statistics dealing with the classification of measurements. More recent contributions stem from research on perceptrons and other "adaptive" decision networks.

1·2   The basic model

We shall assume that each set of data to be classified is a set of d real numbers,* $x_1, x_2, \ldots, x_d$. Such a set we shall call a *pattern*, and we shall call the individual numbers *components* of the pattern. Any device for sorting patterns into categories will be called a *pattern classifier*. In the

---

* In most of what follows, we shall make no restrictions on the values of the real numbers $x_1, x_2, \ldots, x_d$. The few instances in which we assume that they are binary numbers will be explicitly noted.

weather-prediction example discussed previously, we might have $d = 4$ and

$$x_1 = 1023$$
$$x_2 = 1013$$
$$x_3 = 4$$
$$x_4 = -7$$

These four numbers might be the current atmospheric pressures (in millibars) at stations 1 and 2 and the pressure changes at these stations, respectively.

Suppose that there are R categories into which the patterns must be sorted. We shall label these categories by the integers 1, 2, . . . , R. One of these integers, perhaps R, might correspond to a "reject" or "null" category. Thus, in our weather-forecasting example we might have $R = 3$ and the following:

Category	Prediction
1	Rain tomorrow
2	No rain tomorrow
3	Undecided

We shall adopt as our basic model of a pattern classifier a device with d input lines and one output line (see Fig. 1·1). The d input lines are activated simultaneously by the pattern, and the output line responds*

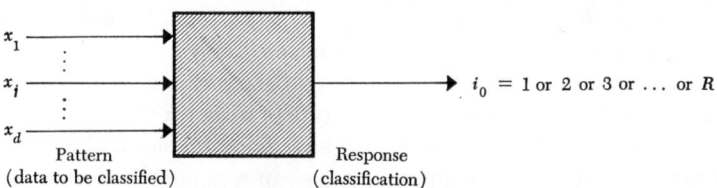

FIGURE 1·1   A pattern classifier

with a signal i_0 which may have one of R distinct values. Each value of the response represents a category into which a pattern may be placed, and we shall accordingly label the response values by the integers 1, . . . , R.

It is the purpose of this chapter to develop further this basic model and to introduce two philosophies for the design of pattern classifiers. First, however, a few words are in order about a key assumption under-

---

* We assume that the response is a deterministic (nonrandom) function of the input pattern. Pattern classifiers with random responses have been discussed occasionally in the literature, but our treatment shall not include them.

4 TRAINABLE PATTERN CLASSIFIERS

lying the model, namely that the data to be classified consist of a finite set of real numbers.

1·3 The problem of what to measure

In assuming that the data to be classified consist of d real numbers, we are obliged to mention, at least briefly, the difficulties that attend selecting these numbers from any given physical situation. Before operating a pattern classifier to forecast the weather, we must first decide which d measurements to use as the input pattern. If d can be very large, we might not need to exercise much care in the selection of measurements because it is likely that most of the important ones can be included. But in the more usual and practical cases, in which (for economic reasons) d is smaller than we might like it to be, the problem of measurement selection is a pressing one.

Unfortunately, there is very little theory to guide our selection of measurements. At worst this selection process is guided solely by the designer's intuitive ideas about which measurements play an important role in the classification to be performed. At best the process can make use of known information about some measurements that are certain to be important. A weather forecaster in the northern hemisphere might know, for example, that he must look to the west to gather the most important measurements on which to base a forecast.

It is beyond the scope of this book to discuss the problems of measurement selection in greater detail. Most of the measurement-selection techniques that have been developed are specific to a particular application and thus would not be appropriate topics in a general treatment such as this. We shall henceforth assume that the d measurements yielding the pattern to be classified have been selected as wisely as possible while remembering that the pattern classifier cannot itself compensate for a careless selection of measurements.

1·4 Decision surfaces in pattern space

Let us return now to the development of our pattern-classifier model. Some of the interesting properties of this model can be conveniently discussed in geometric terms. Any pattern can be represented by a point in a d-dimensional Euclidean space E^d called the *pattern space*. The rectangular coordinates of the point are the real numbers $x_1, x_2, \ldots$, and x_d. The vector **X** extending from the origin to the point $(x_1, x_2, \ldots, x_d)$ can also be used to represent the pattern. The components of **X** are the same numbers $x_1, x_2, \ldots, x_d$. We shall denote both the pattern point and the pattern vector by the symbol **X**.

A pattern classifier is thus a device which maps the points of E^d into the category numbers, $1, \ldots, R$. Let the symbol $\mathcal{R}_i$ denote the set of

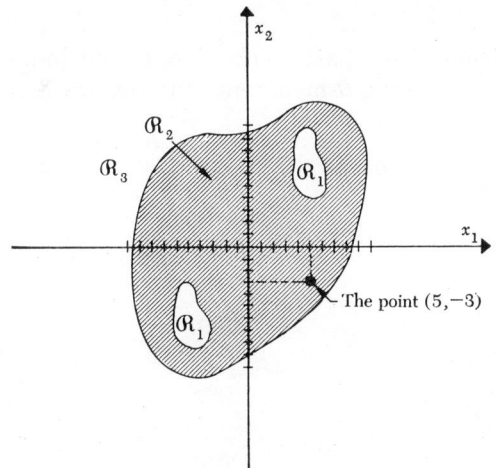

FIGURE 1·2 Point sets in E^2 which map into category numbers

points in E^d which are mapped into the number i. Then, for each category number, we have a set of points in E^d denoted by one of the symbols $\mathcal{R}_1, \mathcal{R}_2, \ldots, \mathcal{R}_R$. As an example, consider the sets shown in Fig. 1·2 where $d = 2$ and $R = 3$. A point in the plane is mapped into the numbers 1, 2, or 3, according to its membership in $\mathcal{R}_1$, $\mathcal{R}_2$, or $\mathcal{R}_3$, respectively. For example, the pattern $(5, -3)$ would be placed in category 2.

Note that the point sets of Fig. 1·2 are separated from each other by surfaces (curves in E^2) called *decision surfaces*. We shall not consider in this book any mappings requiring an infinite number of decision surfaces or any mappings that cannot be described by such surfaces.* In general,

---

* The mapping which takes all points having one or more irrational coordinates into category 1 and all other points (i.e., points all of whose coordinates are rational) into category 2 is an example of a mapping outside the range of our consideration. In assuming that a mapping can be described by a finite number of boundary surfaces, we are making the basic assumption that for almost all points in E^d a slight motion of the point does not change the category of the point. For most physical problems this seems a fair assumption to make.

the decision surfaces divide E^d into R regions which we shall call *decision regions*. The ith region $\mathcal{R}_i$ is the set of points which map into the ith category number. For convenience, we shall arbitrarily assume that patterns which lie *on* decision surfaces do not belong to any of the decision regions; the response of the pattern classifier to such patterns shall be undefined.

1·5 Discriminant functions

The decision surfaces of any pattern classifier can be implicitly defined by a set of functions containing R members. Let $g_1(\mathbf{X}), g_2(\mathbf{X}), \ldots, g_R(\mathbf{X})$ be

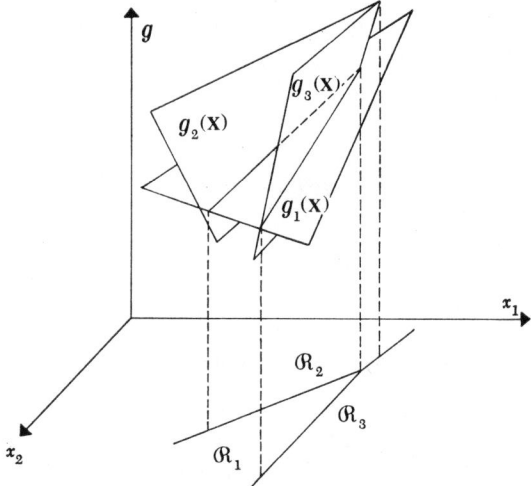

FIGURE 1·3 Examples of discriminant functions for two-dimensional patterns

scalar and single-valued functions of the pattern $\mathbf{X}$. These functions, which we call *discriminant functions*, are chosen such that for all $\mathbf{X}$ in $\mathcal{R}_i$, $g_i(\mathbf{X}) > g_j(\mathbf{X})$ for $i, j = 1, \ldots, R, j \neq i$. That is, in $\mathcal{R}_i$, the ith discriminant function has the largest value. We also assume that discriminant functions are continuous across the decision surfaces; then the decision surface separating contiguous regions $\mathcal{R}_i$ and $\mathcal{R}_j$ is given by

$$g_i(\mathbf{X}) - g_j(\mathbf{X}) = 0 \tag{1·1}$$

Figure 1·3 illustrates three discriminant functions and the decision regions that they imply in the x_1, x_2 plane. Note that the decision surfaces in the x_1, x_2 plane are given by the projections of the intersections of the discriminant functions. Of course, the location and form of the decision surfaces do not uniquely specify the discriminant functions. For one thing, the same arbitrary constant can be added to each discriminant function without altering the implied decision surfaces. In general, any monotonic nondecreasing function (e.g., logarithmic) can be used to convert a set of given discriminant functions into an equivalent set.

The notion of discriminant functions is a useful one primarily because it suggests a convenient and familiar, if not unique, method by which decision surfaces can be implemented. The following exposition of this

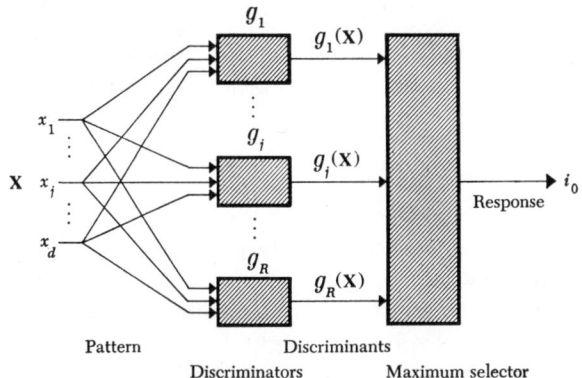

FIGURE 1·4 Basic model for a pattern classifier

method will produce a more detailed functional block diagram of the basic model for a pattern classifier discussed in Sec. 1·2. Our discriminant-function pattern classifier, illustrated in Fig. 1·4, would employ R *discriminators*, each of which computes the value of a discriminant function. The outputs of the discriminators will be called *discriminants*. In classifying a pattern $\mathbf{X}$, the R discriminants are compared by a maximum selector which indicates the largest discriminant.

An interesting form results when there are only two categories, $R = 2$. Here, the maximum selector must decide which is the larger, $g_1(\mathbf{X})$ or $g_2(\mathbf{X})$. It turns out that this decision can be implemented by evaluating the *sign* of a single discriminant function $g(\mathbf{X}) \triangleq g_1(\mathbf{X}) - g_2(\mathbf{X})$. If $g(\mathbf{X})$ is positive, $\mathbf{X}$ is placed in category 1; if $g(\mathbf{X})$ is negative, $\mathbf{X}$ is placed in category 2.* The equation $g(\mathbf{X}) = 0$ gives the decision surface sepa-

* Even in the case $R > 2$ the number of discriminant functions can be reduced from R to $R - 1$ by selecting one of them, say $g_1(\mathbf{X})$, and then subtracting $g_1(\mathbf{X})$ from all of the others. Then the pattern classifier will place $\mathbf{X}$ in category 1 if the largest of the resulting discriminants is negative; otherwise it will place $\mathbf{X}$ into the category corresponding to the largest discriminant. For simplicity of exposition we shall always assume that there are actually R discriminant functions (unless $R = 2$)

8 TRAINABLE PATTERN CLASSIFIERS

rating the regions $\mathcal{R}_1$ and $\mathcal{R}_2$. The sign of $g(\mathbf{X})$ can be evaluated by a threshold element whose threshold value is equal to zero. For this reason the threshold element assumes an important role in pattern-classifying machines. We shall use the block diagram of Fig. 1·5 as a basic model of a two-category pattern classifier, which we call a *pattern dichotomizer*.

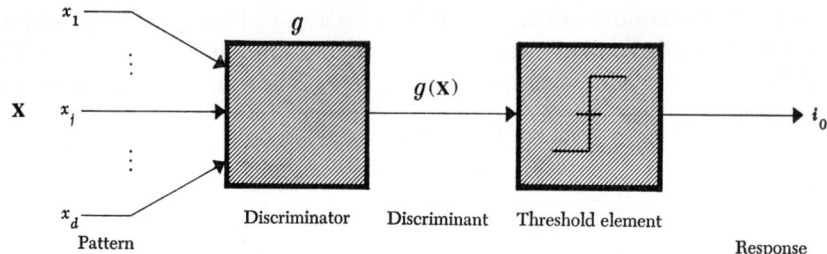

FIGURE 1 · 5   Basic model for a pattern dichotomizer

Using the basic models of Figs. 1·4 and 1·5 we can state that the central problem in the design of pattern classifiers is the specification of the discriminant functions $g_1, g_2, \ldots, g_R$ ($R > 2$) or of the discriminant function g ($R = 2$). In the following sections we shall discuss a class of methods by which this selection might be made.

1 · 6   The selection of discriminant functions

Discriminant functions can be selected in a variety of ways. Sometimes they are calculated with precision on the basis of complete a priori knowledge about the patterns to be classified. At other times reasonable guesses are made on the basis of qualitative knowledge about the patterns. In each of these cases, especially in the second, it may be necessary to "touch up" or adjust the discriminators to achieve acceptable performance on actual patterns. This adjustment process is usually performed by using a set of patterns which are representative of the actual patterns which the machine must classify.* Making a few final adjustments is always an important phase in the design of any equipment. In this book we are interested in those cases in which it is the *major* phase.

* The adjustments can occur after the machine is constructed by making changes in the organization, structure, or parameter values of the parts of the machine, or it can occur before hardware construction by making these changes on a simulated machine using, for example, a digital computer.

We shall assume here that little if any a priori knowledge exists about the patterns to be classified. We might make guesses at discriminant functions, but usually these are very poor indeed. The performance level which the pattern classifier is eventually to achieve must be achieved largely by an adjustment process, which has become known as *training*.

The training process proceeds as follows: a large number of patterns are chosen as typical of those which the machine must ultimately classify. This set of patterns is called the *training set*. The desired classifications of these patterns are assumed to be known. Discriminant functions are then chosen, by methods to be discussed in general below and more specifically later, which perform adequately on the training set. We shall say that these discriminant functions are obtained by *training*. A pattern classifier whose discriminant functions can be obtained by training is called a *trainable pattern classifier*.

1·7 Training methods

In this book we shall discuss examples of two types of training methods, *parametric* and *nonparametric*. The parametric methods are appropriate for classification tasks where each pattern category i, $i = 1, \ldots, R$, is known a priori to be characterized by a set of *parameters*, some of whose values are unknown. If the values of these parameters were known, adequate discriminant functions based on them could be directly specified. In the parametric training methods the training set is used for the purpose of obtaining estimates of the parameter values, and the discriminant functions are then determined by these estimates.

Let us discuss a particular example of the parametric method. Suppose we have two classes of patterns and we wish to design a pattern dichotomizer. It is known a priori that the pattern points in category 1 tend to cluster close to some central cluster point $\mathbf{X}_1$, and that the pattern points in category 2 tend to cluster close to another cluster point $\mathbf{X}_2$. The coordinates of the points $\mathbf{X}_1$ and $\mathbf{X}_2$ constitute the parameters of the pattern sets. The exact values of the coordinates of the points $\mathbf{X}_1$ and $\mathbf{X}_2$ are not known, however. If they were known, it might be reasonable for the pattern classifier to divide the pattern space into two regions $\mathfrak{R}_1$ and $\mathfrak{R}_2$ by some simple decision surface such as a hyperplane. A useful hyperplane might be one which bisects and is normal to the line joining $\mathbf{X}_1$ and $\mathbf{X}_2$. A discriminant function which would implement this kind of separation is

$$g(\mathbf{X}) = (\mathbf{X}_1 - \mathbf{X}_2) \cdot \mathbf{X} + \tfrac{1}{2}|\mathbf{X}_2|^2 - \tfrac{1}{2}|\mathbf{X}_1|^2 \qquad (1\cdot2)$$

where $\mathbf{A} \cdot \mathbf{B}$ is the dot or scalar product of the vectors $\mathbf{A}$ and $\mathbf{B}$, and $|\mathbf{A}|^2 = \mathbf{A} \cdot \mathbf{A}$ is the squared magnitude of the vector $\mathbf{A}$. The hyperplane decision surface $g(\mathbf{X}) = 0$ is illustrated in Fig. 1·6 for the case $d = 2$.

The parametric training method in this case would use the training set to derive estimates of $\mathbf{X}_1$ and $\mathbf{X}_2$. Suppose the training set consisted of N_1 patterns belonging to category 1 and N_2 patterns belonging to category 2. Reasonable estimates for $\mathbf{X}_1$ and $\mathbf{X}_2$ might then be the respective sample means (centers of gravity) of the patterns in each category. Once

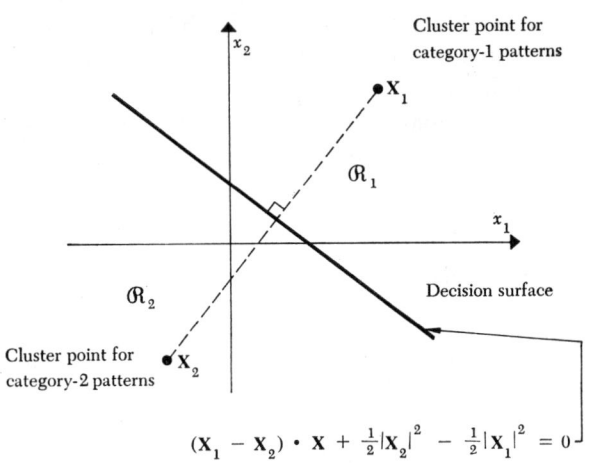

FIGURE 1·6 A linear decision surface based on parameters of the pattern sets

these sample means were estimated, Eq. (1·2) could be used for the specification of $g(\mathbf{X})$, and the parametric training process would be completed.

The nonparametric training methods are most appropriately applied when no assumptions can be made about characterizing parameters. In the usual applications of these methods, functional *forms* are assumed for the discriminant functions such as linear, quadric, or piecewise linear (to be discussed later). These forms have unspecified coefficients which are adjusted or set in such a way that the discriminant functions perform adequately on the training set. For example, we might decide to use a linear discriminant function of the form

$$g(\mathbf{X}) = w_1 x_1 + w_2 x_2 + \cdots + w_d x_d + w_{d+1}$$

in a two-category pattern classifier. The equation $g(\mathbf{X}) = 0$ gives a hyperplane which is the decision surface. The training process is then one of adjusting the coefficients $(w_1, w_2, \ldots, w_d, w_{d+1})$ so that the decision surface implements an acceptable separation of the two classes of patterns in the training set.

1·8 Summary of book by chapters

In the next chapter we discuss several families of discriminant functions as possible candidates for use in a pattern-classifying machine. We examine the properties of some in detail, and present block diagrams to suggest the manner in which they might be employed.

Chapter 3 will investigate decision-theoretic parametric training methods. The mathematical foundation underlying these training methods seems to be more extensive than the theory supporting the nonparametric training methods. On the other hand, employment of decision-theoretic methods presently requires restrictive assumptions about the nature of the pattern classes. These assumptions are not necessary for the use of some of the nonparametric methods.

In Chapter 4 we begin our discussion of examples of some of the nonparametric training methods. There we shall introduce some of the more important training algorithms currently in use. The presentation will be accompanied by geometrical representations which can enhance understanding of the concepts underlying these algorithms.

Theorems about the convergence properties of the nonparametric training algorithms are stated and proved in Chapter 5. These theorems apply to a large class of discriminant functions and are therefore of fundamental importance.

The concept of a layered machine is introduced in Chapter 6. Most of the pattern classifiers containing threshold elements that have been proposed are layered machines. While there is only a scanty mathematical understanding of these machines, two complementary viewpoints are discussed which aid formulation of meaningful questions. Unfortunately, the discriminant functions employed by layered machines do not belong to the class of functions for which the theorems of Chapter 5 apply; nevertheless, there do exist some useful training procedures for layered machines which shall be discussed.

Chapter 7 treats machines with piecewise linear decision surfaces. Some of the training methods suggested for these machines appear to avoid certain disadvantages inherent in the training methods introduced in Chapters 4 and 6.

1·9 Bibliographical and historical remarks

A comprehensive survey of early work on trainable pattern-classifying machines has been written by Hawkins.[1] Sebestyen[2] identifies the task of finding "clustering" transformations as central to the design of pattern classifiers. A paper by Kanal et al.[3] contains an excellent formulation of the pattern-classification problem and also points out that many schemes currently attracting the attention of engineers have antecedents in the statistical literature.

The problem of data classification has indeed received much attention by statisticians. A report by Harley et al.[4] contains an excellent summary (by Kanal) of statistical methods for pattern classification. Of the many sources referenced in that summary we might mention the books of Fisher[5] and Rao.[6] Anderson[7] also deals with the application of statistical techniques to classification problems.

The problem of selection of measurements has also received some attention by both statisticians and engineers. Bahadur,[8] Lewis,[9] and Marill and Green[10] propose and discuss tests for the "effectiveness" of measurements. Miller[11] illustrates a method for selecting a small number of "good" measurements from a larger pool of measurements. Block, Nilsson, and Duda[12] describe a method for determining *features* of patterns. Some specific examples of measurement devices for optical character recognition are discussed in a book edited by Fischer et al.[13] Reports by Brain et al.[14] discuss the development of "optical preprocessors" for visual data.

REFERENCES

1 Hawkins, J.: Self-organizing Systems: A Review and Commentary, *Proc. IRE*, vol. 49, no. 1, pp. 31–48, January, 1961.
2 Sebestyen, G.: "Decision-making Processes in Pattern Recognition," The Macmillan Company, New York, 1962.
3 Kanal, L., et al.: Basic Principles of Some Pattern Recognition Systems, *Proc. National Electronics Conference*, vol. 18, pp. 279–295, October, 1962.
4 Harley, T., et al.: Semi-automatic Imagery Screening Research Study and Experimental Investigation, *Philco Reports* VO43-2 and VO43-3, vol. I, sec. 6, and Appendix H, prepared for U.S. Army Electronics Research and

Development Laboratory under Contract DA-36-039-SC-90742, March 29, 1963.
5 Fisher, R. A.: "Contributions to Mathematical Statistics," John Wiley & Sons, Inc., New York, 1952.
6 Rao, C. R.: "Advanced Statistical Methods in Biometric Research," John Wiley & Sons, Inc., New York, 1952.
7 Anderson, T. W.: "Introduction to Multivariate Statistical Analysis," chap. 6, John Wiley & Sons, Inc., New York, 1958.
8 Bahadur, R. R.: On Classification Based on Responses to n Dichotomous Items, in H. Solomon (ed.), "Studies in Item Analysis and Prediction," Stanford University Press, Stanford, California, 1961.
9 Lewis, P. M.: The Characteristic Selection Problem in Recognition Systems, *Trans. IRE on Info. Theory*, vol. IT-8, no. 2, pp. 171–178, February, 1962.
10 Marill, T., and D. M. Green: On the Effectiveness of Receptors in Recognition Systems, *Trans. IEEE on Info. Theory*, vol. IT-9, no. 1, pp. 11–17, January, 1963.
11 Miller, R. G.: "Statistical Prediction by Discriminant Analysis," *Meteorological Monographs*, vol. 4, no. 25, American Meteorological Society, Boston, Massachusetts, October, 1962.
12 Block, H. D., N. J. Nilsson and R. O. Duda: Determination and Detection of Features in Patterns, in J. Tou and R. Wilcox (eds.), "Computer and Information Sciences," Spartan Books, Washington, D.C., 1964.
13 Fischer, G. L., Jr., et al.: "Optical Character Recognition," Spartan Books, Washington, D.C., 1962.
14 Brain, A. E., et al.: Graphical Data Processing Research Study and Experimental Investigation, *Reports* 7, 8, 9, and 13, prepared for U.S. Army Signal Research and Development Laboratory under Contract DA 36-039-SC-78343 and continuation, 1962 and 1963.

CHAPTER 2

SOME IMPORTANT DISCRIMINANT FUNCTIONS: THEIR PROPERTIES AND THEIR IMPLEMENTATIONS

2·1 Families of discriminant functions

The task of selecting a discriminant function for use in a pattern-classifying machine is simplified by first limiting the class of functions from which the selection is to be made. For this reason we consider *families* of discriminant functions. A discriminant function family can be defined through the use of *parameters* whose values determine the members of the family. For example, suppose a discriminant function $g(\mathbf{X})$ depends also on the values of M real parameters $w_1, w_2, \ldots, w_M$. We make this dependence explicit by writing $g(\mathbf{X})$ in the form

$$g(\mathbf{X}) = g(\mathbf{X}; w_1, w_2, \ldots, w_M) \qquad (2\cdot1)$$

The set of functions that can be obtained by varying the values of the parameters, throughout their ranges, is called a *family* of functions.

16 SOME IMPORTANT DISCRIMINANT FUNCTIONS

A particular function belonging to this family can be selected by choosing the appropriate values of the parameters. The training of a machine restricted to employ discriminant functions belonging to a particular family can then be accomplished by adjusting the values of the parameters. We shall often call these parameters *weights*. In this book we shall be interested in only those pattern-classifying machines whose discriminant functions are obtained by selecting or adjusting the values of weights.

Here we shall define several families of discriminant functions and study their properties, leaving the subject of training to later chapters. One of the simplest is the family of linear functions to which we now turn.

2·2 Linear discriminant functions

Let us consider first the family of discriminant functions of the form

$$g(\mathbf{X}) = w_1 x_1 + w_2 x_2 + \cdots + w_d x_d + w_{d+1} \qquad (2 \cdot 2)$$

This function is a linear function of the components of $\mathbf{X}$; we shall denote discriminant functions of this form by the term *linear discriminant function*. A complete specification of any linear discriminant function is achieved by specifying the values of the weights or parameters of the function family.

A pattern classifier employing linear discriminant functions can be simply implemented using weighting and summing devices as discriminators. Such a machine, termed a *linear machine*, is depicted in Fig. 2·1. In Fig. 2·1 we employ the notation w_{ij} to represent the coefficient of x_j in the ith linear discriminant function. An important special case of a linear machine is a minimum-distance classifier with respect to points. We shall consider this special case first before discussing the properties of linear machines in general.

2·3 Minimum-distance classifiers

Suppose we are given the R points $\mathbf{P}_1, \mathbf{P}_2, \ldots, \mathbf{P}_R$ in E^d. The Euclidean distance between an arbitrary point $\mathbf{X}$ and $\mathbf{P}_i$ is given by

$$|\mathbf{X} - \mathbf{P}_i| = \sqrt{(\mathbf{X} - \mathbf{P}_i) \cdot (\mathbf{X} - \mathbf{P}_i)} \qquad (2 \cdot 3)$$

SOME IMPORTANT DISCRIMINANT FUNCTIONS

Associated with each point $\mathbf{P}_i$ is a category number i, $i = 1, \ldots, R$. A *minimum-distance classifier*, with respect to the points $\mathbf{P}_1, \mathbf{P}_2, \ldots, \mathbf{P}_R$, places each point $\mathbf{X}$ into that category i_0 which is associated with the nearest point $\mathbf{P}_{i_0}$ of the points $\mathbf{P}_1, \mathbf{P}_2, \ldots, \mathbf{P}_R$. That is, for any $\mathbf{X}$, the quantities $|\mathbf{X} - \mathbf{P}_i|$, $i = 1, \ldots, R$ are calculated, and $\mathbf{X}$ is placed into the category associated with the smallest. The points $\mathbf{P}_1, \mathbf{P}_2, \ldots, \mathbf{P}_R$ are called *prototype points*.

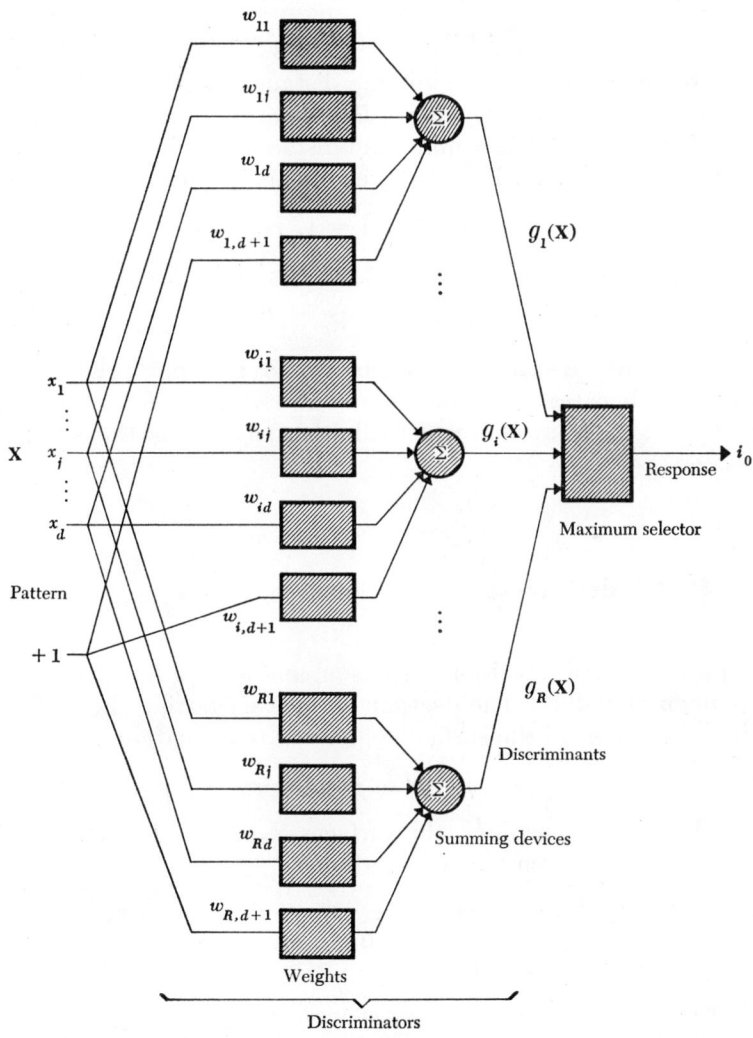

FIGURE 2·1 A linear machine

SOME IMPORTANT DISCRIMINANT FUNCTIONS

An equivalent classification is obtained by comparing the squared distances $|\mathbf{X} - \mathbf{P}_i|^2$, $i = 1, \ldots, R$. Squaring both sides of Eq. (2·3) we obtain

$$|\mathbf{X} - \mathbf{P}_i|^2 = (\mathbf{X} - \mathbf{P}_i) \cdot (\mathbf{X} - \mathbf{P}_i) = \mathbf{X} \cdot \mathbf{X} - 2\mathbf{X} \cdot \mathbf{P}_i + \mathbf{P}_i \cdot \mathbf{P}_i \quad (2\cdot 4)$$

The minimum-distance classification can be effected by comparing the expressions $\mathbf{X} \cdot \mathbf{P}_i - \tfrac{1}{2}\mathbf{P}_i \cdot \mathbf{P}_i$ for $i = 1, \ldots, R$ and selecting the largest. It is clear that the discriminant functions in this case can be given by

$$g_i(\mathbf{X}) = \mathbf{X} \cdot \mathbf{P}_i - \tfrac{1}{2}\mathbf{P}_i \cdot \mathbf{P}_i \quad \text{for } i = 1, \ldots, R \quad (2\cdot 5)$$

We conclude that a minimum-distance classifier is a linear machine. Suppose that the components of $\mathbf{P}_i$ are $p_{i1}, p_{i2}, \ldots, p_{id}$. Then the linear machine of Fig. 2·1 is a minimum-distance classifier with respect to the points $\mathbf{P}_1, \mathbf{P}_2, \ldots, \mathbf{P}_R$ if the weights are given the values

$$w_{ij} = p_{ij} \quad \begin{array}{l} i = 1, \ldots, R \\ j = 1, \ldots, d \end{array}$$

and

$$w_{i,d+1} = -\tfrac{1}{2}\mathbf{P}_i \cdot \mathbf{P}_i \quad i = 1, \ldots, R \quad (2\cdot 6)$$

Minimum-distance classifiers would be appropriate in situations where each category is represented by a single prototype pattern $\mathbf{P}_i$, $i = 1, \ldots, R$, around which all other patterns in the category tend to cluster.*

2·4 The decision surfaces of linear machines

Suppose that two decision regions $\mathcal{R}_i$ and $\mathcal{R}_j$ of a linear machine share a common boundary. The decision surface separating these two regions is then a segment of the surface S_{ij} having the equation

$$g_i(\mathbf{X}) - g_j(\mathbf{X}) = 0 \quad (2\cdot 7)$$

For linear machines, the surfaces S_{ij}, $i, j = 1, \ldots, R$, $i \neq j$, are linear surfaces given by the equations

$$(w_{i1} - w_{j1})x_1 + (w_{i2} - w_{j2})x_2 + \cdots + (w_{id} - w_{jd})x_d$$
$$+ (w_{i,d+1} - w_{j,d+1}) = 0 \quad \text{for } i, j = 1, \ldots, R, i \neq j \quad (2\cdot 8)$$

---

* The dot product operation of Eq. (2·5), performed by a minimum-distance classifier, is sometimes called *template matching*. This usage derives from optical methods for image classification. The terms *correlation detection* and *matched filtering* are also used to describe this operation.

SOME IMPORTANT DISCRIMINANT FUNCTIONS   19

There are $R(R-1)/2$ such equations and thus the same number of surfaces S_{ij}. For $d = 2$, a linear surface is called a line; for $d = 3$, a plane; and for $d > 3$, a hyperplane. Thus, the decision surfaces of a linear machine are segments of at most $R(R-1)/2$ hyperplanes.

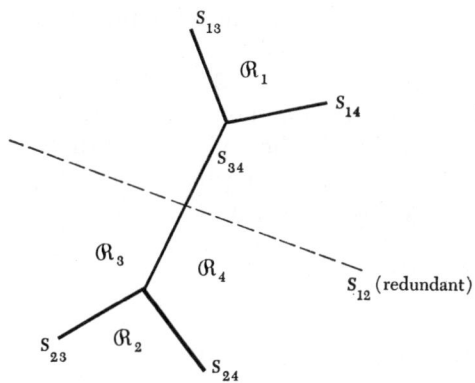

FIGURE 2·2   Examples of decision regions and surfaces resulting from linear discriminant functions

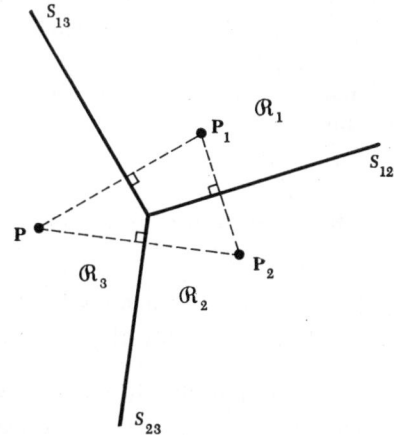

FIGURE 2·3   Decision regions for a minimum-distance classifier with respect to the points P_1, P_2, and P_3

In many cases some of the hyperplanes defined by Eq. (2·8) are not actually used as decision surfaces. The hyperplane S_{ij} is not used if $\mathcal{R}_i$ and $\mathcal{R}_j$ are not contiguous. Such hyperplanes are called *redundant*. Figure 2·2 is an example showing some linear-machine decision regions and surfaces for a case in which $d = 2$ and $R = 4$. Note that the decision surfaces are segments of hyperplanes (lines for $d = 2$), and that S_{12} is redundant. In the special case in which the linear machine is a minimum-distance classifier, the surface S_{ij} is the hyperplane which is the perpendicular bisector of the line segment joining the points $\mathbf{P}_i$ and $\mathbf{P}_j$. Figure 2·3 shows the decision regions and surfaces for the minimum-distance classifier with respect to the two-dimensional points $\mathbf{P}_1$, $\mathbf{P}_2$, and $\mathbf{P}_3$.

We note in the examples of Figs. 2·2 and 2·3 that the decision regions are *convex* (a region is convex if and only if the straight-line segment connecting two arbitrary points in the region lies entirely within the region). It will be left as an exercise for the reader to verify that the decision regions of a linear machine are always convex.

2·5 Linear classifications of patterns

Suppose we have a finite set $\mathfrak{X}$ of distinct patterns $\{\mathbf{X}_1, \mathbf{X}_2, \ldots, \mathbf{X}_N\}$, N in number. Let the patterns of $\mathfrak{X}$ be classified in such a way that each pattern in $\mathfrak{X}$ belongs to only one of R categories. This classification divides $\mathfrak{X}$ into the subsets $\mathfrak{X}_1, \mathfrak{X}_2, \ldots, \mathfrak{X}_R$ such that each pattern in $\mathfrak{X}_i$ belongs to category i for $i = 1, \ldots, R$.

If a linear machine can place each of the patterns in $\mathfrak{X}$ into the proper categories we say that the classification of $\mathfrak{X}$ is a *linear* classification and that the subsets $\mathfrak{X}_1, \mathfrak{X}_2, \ldots, \mathfrak{X}_R$ are *linearly separable*. Stated another way, a classification of $\mathfrak{X}$ is linear and the subsets $\mathfrak{X}_1, \mathfrak{X}_2, \ldots, \mathfrak{X}_R$ are linearly separable if and only if linear discriminant functions $g_1, g_2, \ldots, g_R$ exist such that

$$
\begin{array}{ll}
g_i(\mathbf{X}) > g_j(\mathbf{X}) & \text{for all } \mathbf{X} \text{ in } \mathfrak{X}_i \\
j = 1, \ldots, R, j \neq i & \text{for all } i = 1, \ldots, R
\end{array} \quad (2\cdot 9)
$$

As a special case of the above definition let $R = 2$. We say that a dichotomy of $\mathfrak{X}$ into two subsets $\mathfrak{X}_1$ and $\mathfrak{X}_2$ is a linear dichotomy if and only if a linear discriminant function g exists such that

$$
\begin{array}{ll}
g(\mathbf{X}) > 0 & \text{for all } \mathbf{X} \text{ in } \mathfrak{X}_1 \\
g(\mathbf{X}) < 0 & \text{for all } \mathbf{X} \text{ in } \mathfrak{X}_2
\end{array} \quad (2\cdot 10)
$$

Clearly $\mathfrak{X}_1$ and $\mathfrak{X}_2$ are linearly separable if and only if a hyperplane exists which has each member of $\mathfrak{X}_1$ on one side and each member of $\mathfrak{X}_2$ on the other side.

Because the decision regions of a linear machine are convex, it is easy to show that if the subsets $\mathfrak{X}_1, \mathfrak{X}_2, \ldots, \mathfrak{X}_R$ are linearly separable, then each *pair* of subsets $\mathfrak{X}_i, \mathfrak{X}_j, i, j = 1, \ldots, R, i \neq j$, is also linearly separable. That is, if $\mathfrak{X}_1, \mathfrak{X}_2, \ldots, \mathfrak{X}_R$ are linearly separable, then $\mathfrak{X}_1, \mathfrak{X}_2, \ldots, \mathfrak{X}_R$ are also *pairwise linearly separable*.

2·6 The threshold logic unit (TLU)

If $R = 2$, a linear machine employs a single linear discriminant function $g(\mathbf{X})$ defined by

$$g(\mathbf{X}) = w_1 x_1 + w_2 x_2 + \cdots + w_d x_d + w_{d+1} \qquad (2 \cdot 11)$$

If $g(\mathbf{X}) > 0$, $i_0 = 1$; if $g(\mathbf{X}) < 0$, $i_0 = 2$. The decision regions $\mathcal{R}_1$ and $\mathcal{R}_2$ are separated by a hyperplane decision surface defined by $g(\mathbf{X}) = 0$.

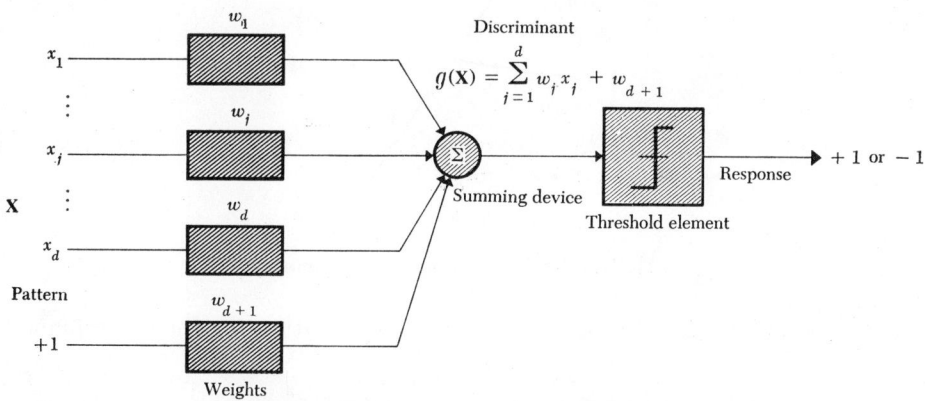

FIGURE 2·4 The threshold logic unit (TLU)

The pattern dichotomizer with linear $g(\mathbf{X})$ can be implemented according to the block diagram in Fig. 2·4. Such a structure, consisting of weights, summing device, and threshold element, is called a *threshold logic unit* (TLU). We shall ordinarily assume that the threshold element is a device which responds with a $+1$ signal if $g(\mathbf{X}) > 0$ and a -1 signal if $g(\mathbf{X}) < 0$. We must then associate a TLU output of $+1$ with pattern category 1 and a TLU output of -1 with pattern category 2. The last term in $g(\mathbf{X})$, w_{d+1}, can be provided by a weight whose value w_{d+1} is energized by a signal of $+1$. Usually this $+1$ signal is associated with the pattern as a $(d+1)$st input x_{d+1}, whose value is always equal to $+1$.

Because the TLU implements a hyperplane decision surface, it is important to list some facts about hyperplane boundaries in order to understand some of the properties of a TLU. Let us define the d-dimensional vector $\mathbf{w}$, with components $w_1, w_2, \ldots, w_d$. The hyperplane equation can then be written as

$$\mathbf{X} \cdot \mathbf{w} = -w_{d+1} \qquad (2\cdot 12)$$

Let $\mathbf{n}$ be a unit vector normal to the hyperplane at some point $\mathbf{P}$ on the hyperplane and directed into the half-space for which $\mathbf{X} \cdot \mathbf{w} > -w_{d+1}$ (see Fig. 2·5). This half-space is called the positive side of the hyperplane.

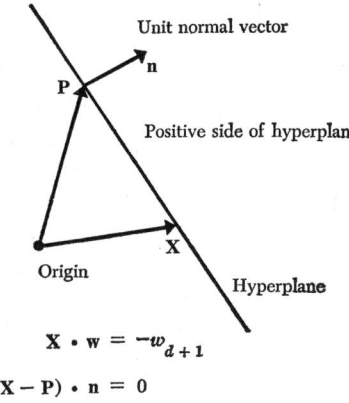

FIGURE 2·5 Hyperplane geometry

From Fig. 2·5 we have an alternative equation for the hyperplane

$$(\mathbf{X} - \mathbf{P}) \cdot \mathbf{n} = 0$$

or $\qquad (2\cdot 13)$

$$\mathbf{X} \cdot \mathbf{n} = \mathbf{P} \cdot \mathbf{n}$$

Dividing Eq. (2·12) by $|\mathbf{w}|$ and then comparing with Eq. (2·13) yields the relations

$$\mathbf{n} = \frac{\mathbf{w}}{|\mathbf{w}|}$$

and $\qquad (2\cdot 14)$

$$\mathbf{n} \cdot \mathbf{P} = -\frac{w_{d+1}}{|\mathbf{w}|}$$

where

$$|\mathbf{w}| = \sqrt{\sum_{i=1}^{d} w_i^2}$$

Note from Fig. 2·5 that the absolute value of $\mathbf{n} \cdot \mathbf{P}$ is the normal Euclidean distance from the origin to the hyperplane. We shall denote this distance by the symbol Δ_w, which we set equal to $w_{d+1}/|\mathbf{w}|$. (If $\Delta_w > 0$, the origin is on the positive side of the hyperplane.)

The equation

$$\mathbf{X} \cdot \mathbf{n} + \Delta_w = 0 \qquad (2\cdot15)$$

is said to be the *normal form* equation of a hyperplane. The direction $\mathbf{n}$ is called the *orientation* of the hyperplane, and the distance Δ_w is called the *position* of the hyperplane.

It is also easy to show that the normal Euclidean distance from the hyperplane to an arbitrary point $\mathbf{X}$ is expressed by

$$\frac{1}{\sqrt{\sum_{i=1}^{d} w_i^2}} (w_1 x_1 + w_2 x_2 + \cdots + w_d x_d + w_{d+1})$$

From our expressions for $\mathbf{n}$ and Δ_w we note the following special cases of interest:

1. If $w_{d+1} = 0$, the hyperplane passes through the origin.
2. If $w_i = 0$ for any $i = 1, \ldots, d$, the hyperplane is parallel to the ith coordinate axis.

At this point, we can conveniently summarize some of the properties of a TLU:

1. A TLU dichotomizes patterns by a hyperplane decision surface in E^d.
2. The hyperplane has an orientation given by the weight values $w_1, w_2, \ldots, w_d$.
3. The hyperplane has a position proportional to w_{d+1}.
4. The distance from the hyperplane to an arbitrary pattern $\mathbf{X}$ is proportional to the value of $g(\mathbf{X})$.

The TLU has been used as the elemental building block of many pattern-classifying machines. Some of these will be considered in detail in Chapter 6.

2·7 Piecewise linear discriminant functions

As a special case of discriminant functions which we shall call *piecewise linear*, we shall first consider those of a minimum-distance classifier with respect to point sets.

Suppose we are given R finite point sets $\mathcal{P}_1, \mathcal{P}_2, \ldots, \mathcal{P}_R$. For each $i = 1, \ldots, R$, let the ith point set consist of the L_i points $\mathbf{P}_i^{(1)}, \mathbf{P}_i^{(2)}, \ldots, \mathbf{P}_i^{(L_i)}$. Let us define the Euclidean distance $d(\mathbf{X}, \mathcal{P}_i)$ from an arbitrary point $\mathbf{X}$ to the point set $\mathcal{P}_i$ by

$$d(\mathbf{X}, \mathcal{P}_i) = \min_{j=1,\ldots,L_i} |\mathbf{X} - \mathbf{P}_i^{(j)}| \qquad (2 \cdot 16)$$

That is, the distance between $\mathbf{X}$ and $\mathcal{P}_i$ is the smallest of the distances between $\mathbf{X}$ and each point in $\mathcal{P}_i$. Let us associate with each set $\mathcal{P}_i$ a category number i for $i = 1, \ldots, R$. We define a *minimum-distance classifier* with respect to the point sets $\mathcal{P}_1, \mathcal{P}_2, \ldots, \mathcal{P}_R$ as one which places each pattern $\mathbf{X}$ into the category associated with the closest point set.

For each $i = 1, \ldots, R$, we define the functions

$$g_i(\mathbf{X}) = \max_{j=1,\ldots,L_i} \{\mathbf{P}_i^{(j)} \cdot \mathbf{X} - \tfrac{1}{2}\mathbf{P}_i^{(j)} \cdot \mathbf{P}_i^{(j)}\} \qquad (2 \cdot 17)$$

Note that $\{\mathbf{P}_i^{(j)} \cdot \mathbf{X} - \tfrac{1}{2}\mathbf{P}_i^{(j)} \cdot \mathbf{P}_i^{(j)}\}$ will be a maximum for that $\mathbf{P}_i^{(j)}$ in $\mathcal{P}_i$ which is closest to $\mathbf{X}$. Therefore, for any $\mathbf{X}$, the largest of the R discriminants $g_1(\mathbf{X}), \ldots, g_R(\mathbf{X})$ will be the one whose index i_0 is associated with the point set $\mathcal{P}_{i_0}$ closest to $\mathbf{X}$. Thus the $g_i(\mathbf{X})$ given by Eq. (2·17) can be used as discriminant functions in a minimum-distance classifier with respect to point sets. Such a classifier would be appropriate if each pattern category were represented by a finite number of prototype patterns around one or the other of which each of the patterns in the category clustered.

Minimum-distance classifiers with respect to point sets prompt us to consider the general family of discriminant functions of the form

$$g_i(\mathbf{X}) = \max_{j=1,\ldots,L_i} \{g_i^{(j)}(\mathbf{X})\} \qquad i = 1, \ldots, R \qquad (2 \cdot 18)$$

where each $g_i^{(j)}(\mathbf{X})$, called a *subsidiary discriminant function*, is given by an expression of the form

$$g_i^{(j)}(\mathbf{X}) = w_{i1}^{(j)} x_1 + w_{i2}^{(j)} x_2 + \cdots + w_{id}^{(j)} x_d + w^{(j)}_{i,d+1} \qquad (2 \cdot 19)$$

SOME IMPORTANT DISCRIMINANT FUNCTIONS

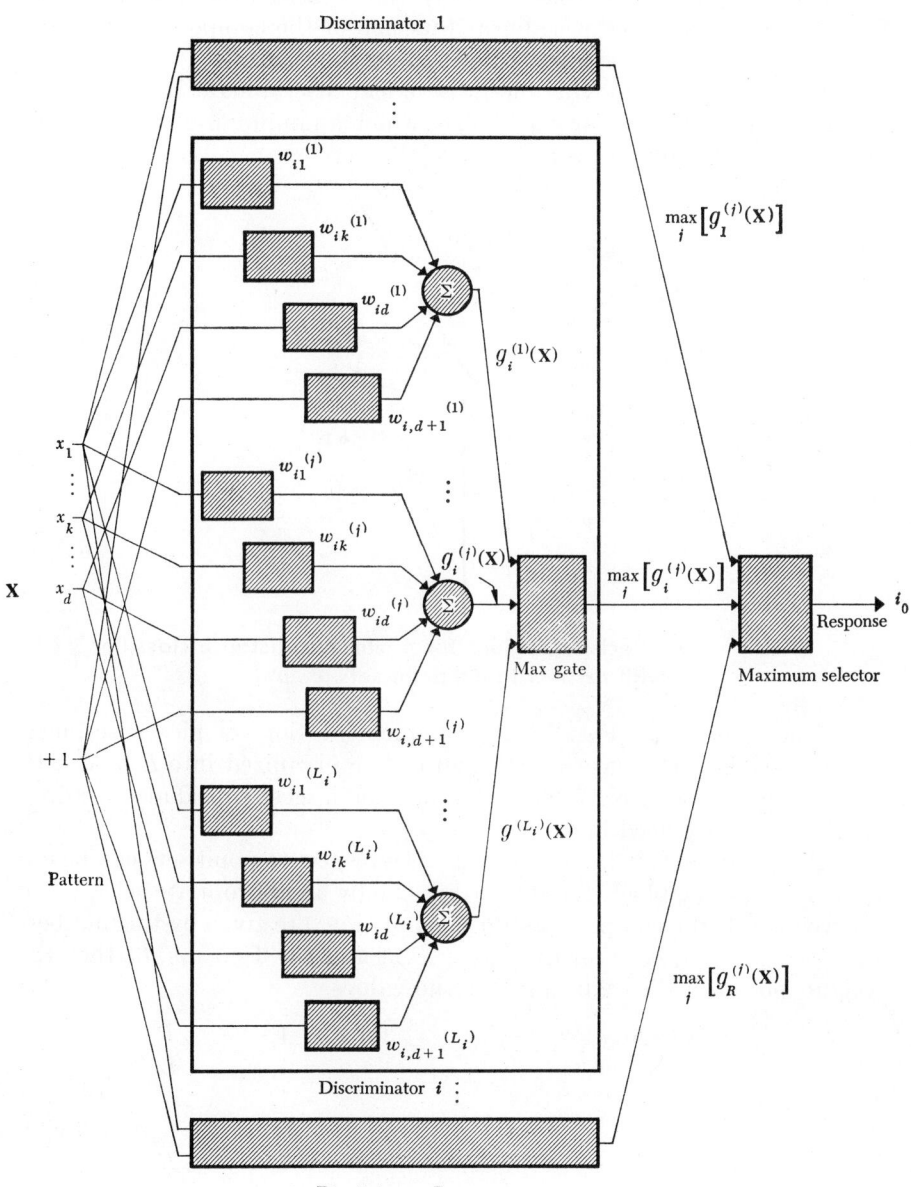

FIGURE 2·6 A piecewise linear machine

26   SOME IMPORTANT DISCRIMINANT FUNCTIONS

where the weights $w_{ik}^{(j)}$, $i = 1, \ldots, R, j = 1, \ldots, L_i, k = 1, \ldots, d + 1$, are the parameters of the family. Since each of these discriminant functions $g_i(\mathbf{X})$ is a piecewise linear function of the components of $\mathbf{X}$ we shall call them *piecewise linear* discriminant functions.*

Any machine employing piecewise linear discriminant functions will be called a piecewise linear machine, of which a minimum-distance classifier with respect to point sets is a special case.

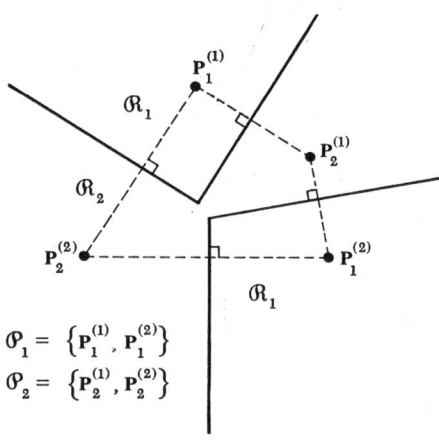

$$\mathcal{P}_1 = \{\mathbf{P}_1^{(1)}, \mathbf{P}_1^{(2)}\}$$
$$\mathcal{P}_2 = \{\mathbf{P}_2^{(1)}, \mathbf{P}_2^{(2)}\}$$

FIGURE 2·7   Decision regions for a minimum-distance classifier with respect to the point sets $\mathcal{P}_1$, $\mathcal{P}_2$

The structure of Fig. 2·6 is an implementation for piecewise linear machines. The subsidiary discriminators are organized into R banks. If, for any pattern $\mathbf{X}$, the ith bank contains the largest subsidiary discriminant, then $\mathbf{X}$ is placed in category i.

The minimum-distance classifier with respect to point sets can be implemented by the block diagram of Fig. 2·6 by an appropriate selection of the weights. If the components of the points $\mathbf{P}_i^{(j)}$ are given by the numbers $p_{i1}^{(j)}, p_{i2}^{(j)}, \ldots, p_{id}^{(j)}$ for $i = 1, \ldots, R$ and $j = 1, \ldots, L_i$, then the weights shown in Fig. 2.6 can have the values

$$w_{ik}^{(j)} = p_{ik}^{(j)} \qquad \text{for } i = 1, \ldots, R$$
$$j = 1, \ldots, L_i$$
$$k = 1, \ldots, d$$

and   (2·20)

$$w^{(j)}_{i,d+1} = -\tfrac{1}{2}\mathbf{P}_i^{(j)} \cdot \mathbf{P}_i^{(j)} \qquad \text{for } i = 1, \ldots, R$$
$$j = 1, \ldots, L_i$$

---

* These are not completely general piecewise linear functions since Eq. (2·18) constrains them to be convex.

SOME IMPORTANT DISCRIMINANT FUNCTIONS

The decision surfaces for piecewise linear machines consist of sections of hyperplanes, just as do those for linear machines. In the piecewise linear case, the decision regions $\Re_1, \ldots, \Re_R$ are not, in general, convex regions.

An example of decision surfaces and regions for $R = 2$ and $d = 2$ is shown in Fig. 2·7 for a minimum-distance classifier with respect to the point sets $\mathcal{P}_1$ and $\mathcal{P}_2$.

2·8 Quadric discriminant functions

A *quadric discriminant* function has the form

$$g_i(\mathbf{X}) = \sum_{j=1}^{d} w_{jj} x_j^2 + \sum_{j=1}^{d-1} \sum_{k=j+1}^{d} w_{jk} x_j x_k + \sum_{j=1}^{d} w_j x_j + w_{d+1} \quad (2\cdot 21)$$

Any machine which employs quadric discriminant functions will be called a *quadric machine*. A quadric discriminant function has $(d+1)(d+2)/2$ parameters or weights consisting of

- d weights as coefficients of x_j^2 terms w_{jj}
- d weights as coefficients of x_j terms w_j
- $d(d-1)/2$ weights as coefficients of $x_j x_k$ terms, $k \neq j$ w_{jk}
- 1 weight which is not a coefficient w_{d+1}

Equation (2·21) can be put into matrix form after making the following definitions. Let the matrix $\mathbf{A} = [a_{jk}]$ have components given by

$$\begin{aligned} a_{jj} &= w_{jj} & j &= 1, \ldots, d \\ a_{jk} &= \tfrac{1}{2} w_{jk} & j, k &= 1, \ldots, d, j \neq k \end{aligned} \quad (2\cdot 22)$$

Let the (column) vector $\mathbf{B} = \begin{pmatrix} b_1 \\ \cdots \\ b_d \end{pmatrix}$ have components given by

$$b_j = w_j \qquad j = 1, \ldots, d \quad (2\cdot 23)$$

Let the scalar $C = w_{d+1}$. Then

$$g(\mathbf{X}) = \mathbf{X}^t \mathbf{A} \mathbf{X} + \mathbf{X}^t \mathbf{B} + C \quad (2\cdot 24)$$

where $\mathbf{X}$ is considered to be a column vector and $\mathbf{X}^t$ denotes the transpose of $\mathbf{X}$ (a row vector).

The term $\mathbf{X}^t \mathbf{A} \mathbf{X}$ is called a *quadratic form*. If all the eigenvalues of $\mathbf{A}$ are positive, the quadratic form is never negative for any vector $\mathbf{X}$ and equal to zero only for $\mathbf{X} = \begin{pmatrix} 0 \\ 0 \\ \cdots \\ 0 \end{pmatrix}$. When these conditions are met, both the matrix **A** and the quadratic form are called *positive definite*. If **A** has one or more of its eigenvalues equal to zero and all the others positive, then the quadratic form will never be negative, and it and **A** are called *positive semidefinite*.

2·9 Quadric decision surfaces

The decision surfaces of quadric machines are sections of second-degree surfaces which we shall call *quadric surfaces*. Specifically, if $\mathcal{R}_i$ and $\mathcal{R}_j$ share a common boundary, it is a section of the surface S_{ij} given by an equation of the form

$$\mathbf{X}^t[\mathbf{A}^{(i)} - \mathbf{A}^{(j)}]\mathbf{X} + \mathbf{X}^t[\mathbf{B}^{(i)} - \mathbf{B}^{(j)}] + [C^{(i)} - C^{(j)}] = 0 \quad (2\cdot25)$$

It is of interest to consider the varieties of quadric surfaces defined by

$$\mathbf{X}^t\mathbf{A}\mathbf{X} + \mathbf{X}^t\mathbf{B} + C = 0 \quad (2\cdot26)$$

If **A** is positive definite, the surface of Eq. (2·26) is called a *hyperellipsoid*. The axes of the hyperellipsoid are in the directions of the eigenvectors of **A**. In the special case in which **A** is an identity (or any scalar) matrix, the surface is called a *hypersphere*.

If **A** is not positive definite but is positive semidefinite, the surface is called a *hyperellipsoidal cylinder*. Cross sections of this cylinder are lower-dimensional hyperellipsoids whose axes are in the directions of the eigenvectors of **A** having nonzero eigenvalues.

If none of the above conditions is fulfilled by **A** (or its negative), the surface is called a *hyperhyperboloid*.

We shall see in Chapter 3 an important application of quadric surfaces.

2·10 Implementation of quadric discriminant functions

There are two important methods of implementing quadric discriminant functions. One is suggested by Eq. (2·21) and will be of importance when we study training procedures. The other implementation can be derived by studying the properties of the matrix **A**. This implementation is of somewhat lesser importance and is discussed in detail in the Appendix.

To explain the more important implementation we first define the M-dimensional vector **F** whose components $f_1, f_2, \ldots, f_M$ are functions of the x_i, $i = 1, \ldots, d$. The first d components of **F** are $x_1^2, x_2^2, \ldots, x_d^2$; the next $d(d-1)/2$ components are all the pairs $x_1 x_2, x_1 x_3, \ldots, x_{d-1} x_d$; the last d components are $x_1, x_2, \ldots, x_d$. The total number of

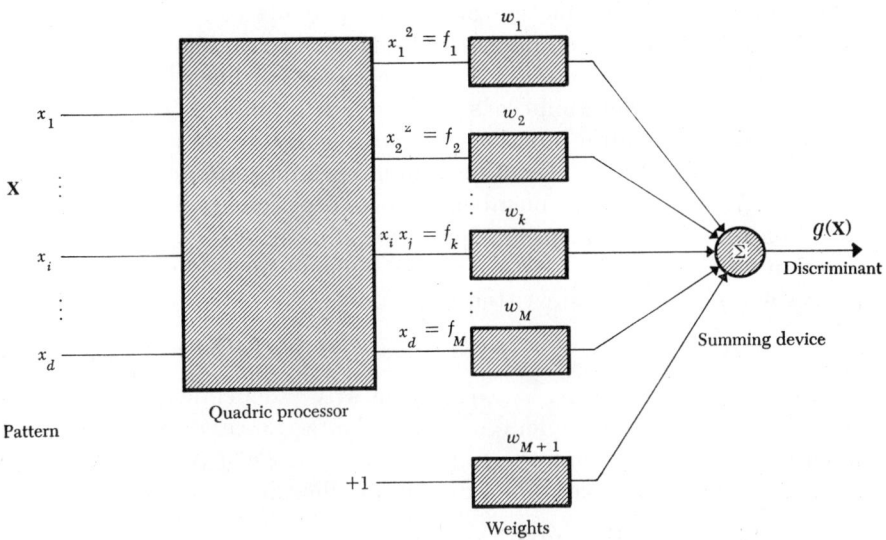

FIGURE 2·8 A quadric discriminator

these components is $M = [d(d+3)]/2$. We shall write this correspondence as

$$\mathbf{F} = \mathbf{F}(\mathbf{X}) \tag{2·27}$$

where $\mathbf{F}(\mathbf{X})$ is a one-to-one transformation. For every **X** in E^d there is a unique **F** in E^M. This one-to-one correspondence allows us to write $g(\mathbf{X})$ as a *linear* function of the components of **F** with the result that for every quadric discriminant function of **X** there corresponds a linear discriminant function of **F**. Equation (2·21) can therefore be written as

$$g(\mathbf{X}) = w_1 f_1 + w_2 f_2 + \cdots + w_M f_M + w_{M+1} \tag{2·28}$$

The implementation of a quadric discriminator, suggested by Eq. (2·28), is shown in Fig. 2·8. It consists of a *quadric processor*, for converting **X** into **F**, followed by weights and a summing device. All variations within the family of quadric discriminant functions can be achieved by varying the weights. A quadric machine can therefore be implemented by a quadric processor followed by a linear machine.

2·11 Φ functions

We noted in Sec. 2·10 that a quadric discriminant function can be considered to be a linear function of the components of a vector $\mathbf{F}$. If we examine Eq. (2·28), which defines the quadric discriminant function, we see that the weights $w_1, w_2, \ldots, w_M, w_{M+1}$ appear linearly. That is, the parameters which determine a specific quadric function from among a whole family of quadric functions appear linearly in the function. There is an important class of function families whose parameters have this property. We shall call the members of these function families Φ functions.

A Φ function, with parameters (weights) $w_1, w_2, \ldots, w_{M+1}$, is a function $\Phi(\mathbf{X}; w_1, w_2, \ldots, w_{M+1})$ which depends linearly on the parameters. A Φ function can be written in the form

$$\Phi(\mathbf{X}) = w_1 f_1(\mathbf{X}) + w_2 f_2(\mathbf{X}) + \cdots + w_M f_M(\mathbf{X}) + w_{M+1} \quad (2\cdot29)$$

where the $f_i(\mathbf{X})$, $i = 1, \ldots, M$, are linearly independent, real, single-valued functions independent of the weights. Since there are $M + 1$ weights we shall say that the number of *degrees of freedom* is equal to $M + 1$. Specific examples of Φ function families are

1. Linear functions: $f_i(\mathbf{X}) = x_i$ for $i = 1, \ldots, d$
2. Quadric functions: $f_i(\mathbf{X})$ is of the form $x_k^n x_l^m$ for

$$k, l = 1, \ldots, d, \quad \text{and} \quad n, m = 0 \text{ and } 1$$

3. rth-order polynomial functions: $f_i(\mathbf{X})$ is of the form

$$x_{k_1}^{n_1} x_{k_2}^{n_2} \ldots x_{k_r}^{n_r} \text{ for}$$

$k_1, k_2, \ldots, k_r = 1, \ldots, d \quad \text{and} \quad n_1, n_2, \ldots, n_r = 0 \text{ and } 1$

In later discussions of the properties of Φ functions we use the notation

$$\mathbf{F}(\mathbf{X}) = \{f_1(\mathbf{X}), f_2(\mathbf{X}), \ldots, f_M(\mathbf{X})\} \quad (2\cdot30)$$

We shall assume that $\mathbf{F}(\mathbf{X})$ is a mapping of $\mathbf{X}$ into a vector $\mathbf{F}$ in an M-dimensional space which we call Φ space. The decision surfaces separating $\mathcal{R}_i$ and $\mathcal{R}_j$ will be called Φ surfaces, if the discriminant functions $g_i(\mathbf{X})$ and $g_j(\mathbf{X})$ are Φ functions. A Φ surface in the pattern space has corresponding to it a hyperplane in the Φ space. Therefore any linear function of $\mathbf{F}$ is a Φ function of $\mathbf{X}$. Many of the results to be presented in this book are developed for linear discriminant functions, but by the above considerations we can extend the application of these results to the whole class of Φ functions. We shall call any pattern-classifying machine employing Φ functions a Φ *machine*. A Φ machine consists of a Φ *processor* (which computes **F** from **X**) followed by a linear machine. Note that piecewise linear machines are not Φ machines since piecewise linear discriminant functions are not linear in their parameters.

2·12 The utility of Φ functions for classifying patterns

Having described some important families of discriminant functions, we now compare the relative utilities of these families. The ultimate test of a discriminant function family is the question: How efficient are the members of this family for use in classifying patterns? In this section we shall

TABLE 2·1   The eight classifications of three patterns

Classification	Pattern categories		
	$\mathbf{X}_1$	$\mathbf{X}_2$	$\mathbf{X}_3$
1	1	1	1
2	1	1	2
3	1	2	1
4	1	2	2
5	2	1	1
6	2	1	2
7	2	2	1
8	2	2	2

formulate and answer a specific question of this nature for the entire class of Φ functions (including linear, quadric, rth-degree polynomial, etc.). We shall restrict our attention to the case $R = 2$.

Suppose we have N patterns represented as points in E^d. Clearly, there exist a total of 2^N distinct classifications of these patterns into two categories (dichotomies); each pattern may independently be assigned to category 1 or category 2. For example, there are eight classifications of the three patterns $\mathbf{X}_1$, $\mathbf{X}_2$, and $\mathbf{X}_3$. These are listed in Table 2·1.

32 SOME IMPORTANT DISCRIMINANT FUNCTIONS

One measure of the effectiveness of a discriminant function family would be the total number of dichotomies of N patterns that its members could effect. We shall show that if the positions of the N pattern points satisfy some quite mild conditions, the number of dichotomies that can be implemented by a Φ function will depend only on the number of patterns N and the number of parameters $M + 1$ of the Φ function, not on the configuration of the patterns or on the form of the Φ function.

2·13 The number of linear dichotomies of N points of d dimensions

We shall begin by calculating the number of dichotomies of N patterns achievable by a linear discriminant function (i.e., a TLU). Recall that each of these dichotomies is called a *linear dichotomy*. For N d-dimensional patterns, let $L(N,d)$ be the number of linear dichotomies. $L(N,d)$ is equal to twice the number of ways in which N points can be partitioned by a $(d - 1)$-dimensional hyperplane. (For each distinct partition, there are two different classifications).

Before obtaining a general expression for $L(N,d)$ consider the case $N = 4$, $d = 2$ as an example. Figure 2·9a shows four points in a two-dimensional space. The lines l_i, $i = 1, \ldots, 7$ effect all possible *linear partitions* of these four points. Consider l_3 in particular. It could be the decision surface implementing either of the following: (1) $\mathbf{X}_1$ and $\mathbf{X}_2$ in category 1, and $\mathbf{X}_3$ and $\mathbf{X}_4$ in category 2; or (2) $\mathbf{X}_3$ and $\mathbf{X}_4$ in category 1, and $\mathbf{X}_1$ and $\mathbf{X}_2$ in category 2.

Note that the exact configuration of the points does not influence the *number*, seven, of linear partitions unless three of the points are collinear (Fig. 2·9b). In the latter case, there are only six linear partitions. For $N > d$, we say that a set of N points is in *general position* in a d-dimensional space if and only if no subset of $d + 1$ points lies on a $(d - 1)$-dimensional hyperplane. When $N \leq d$, a set of N points is in general position if no $(N - 2)$-dimensional hyperplane contains the set. Thus the four points in Fig. 2·9a are in general position, whereas the four points of Fig. 2·9b are not. Unless otherwise noted, we shall always assume that the N points for which we are calculating $L(N,d)$ are in general position.*

---

* In some special cases, important in practice, the pattern points may not be in general position. For example, if the pattern components are binary, the pattern points are the vertices of a hypercube; in this case general position implies that no subset of $d + 1$ vertices may lie on the same $(d - 1)$-dimensional face. Even when the pattern points are not in general position, the derivation to follow yields a useful upper bound on $L(N,d)$.

SOME IMPORTANT DISCRIMINANT FUNCTIONS

Thus, depending only on the condition of general position of the points, and otherwise independent of the configuration of the points, we observe from Fig. 2·9a that $L(4,2) = 2 \cdot 7 = 14$. This number is to be compared with the $2^4 = 16$ total possible dichotomies of four pattern points.

We shall now derive a general expression for $L(N,d)$ by developing a recursion relation which it must satisfy.* Assume that we have a set $\mathfrak{X}'$ of $N - 1$ points $\mathbf{X}_1, \mathbf{X}_2, \ldots, \mathbf{X}_{N-1}$ in general position in E^d. There are $L(N - 1, d)$ linear dichotomies of $\mathfrak{X}'$. We wish to find out by how much this number of linear dichotomies is increased if the set $\mathfrak{X}'$ is enlarged to

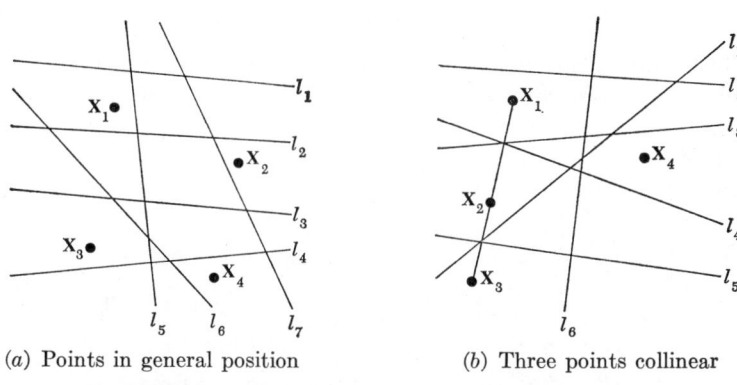

(a) Points in general position (b) Three points collinear

FIGURE 2·9 Linear partitions of four points in E^2

include one more point $\mathbf{X}_N$. Let the enlarged set of N points $\mathbf{X}_1, \mathbf{X}_2, \ldots, \mathbf{X}_N$ be denoted by the symbol $\mathfrak{X}$. The additional point $\mathbf{X}_N$ is chosen so that the points in $\mathfrak{X}$ are in general position in E^d.

Clearly, some of the dichotomies of the smaller set $\mathfrak{X}'$ can be achieved by hyperplanes which pass through the additional point $\mathbf{X}_N$. Let us say that exactly $L_{\mathbf{X}_N}(N - 1, d)$ of the $L(N - 1, d)$ linear dichotomies of the $N - 1$ points in $\mathfrak{X}'$ can be achieved by hyperplanes passing through $\mathbf{X}_N$. Then $L(N - 1, d) - L_{\mathbf{X}_N}(N - 1, d)$ of the linear dichotomies of $\mathfrak{X}'$ cannot be achieved by these constrained hyperplanes. Each of these linear dichotomies of $\mathfrak{X}'$ not achievable by a hyperplane passing through $\mathbf{X}_N$ determines *one* dichotomy of the larger set $\mathfrak{X}$. For each of the linear dichotomies of $\mathfrak{X}'$ that *can* be achieved by a hyperplane passing through $\mathbf{X}_N$, there are *two* possible dichotomies of $\mathfrak{X}$: one for which $\mathbf{X}_N$ is placed in

---

* In some of the derivations to follow in this and subsequent sections, we shall use some facts from geometry which, while obvious for two- and three-dimensional spaces, happen to be valid in any finite-dimensional space. Of course, each of these derivations could also be given in algebraic form, but with the disadvantage of a more cumbersome presentation.

SOME IMPORTANT DISCRIMINANT FUNCTIONS

category 1, and one for which $\mathbf{X}_N$ is placed in category 2. (That is, for these dichotomies, $\mathbf{X}_N$ can be arbitrarily classified by a slight motion of the hyperplane.)* Clearly, then, the total number of linear dichotomies of the complete set $\mathfrak{X}$ is given by

$$L(N,d) = L(N-1, d) - L_{\mathbf{x}_N}(N-1, d) + 2L_{\mathbf{x}_N}(N-1, d)$$
$$= L(N-1, d) + L_{\mathbf{x}_N}(N-1, d) \tag{2.31}$$

where $L_{\mathbf{x}_N}(N-1, d)$ = the number of linear dichotomies of $N-1$ points achievable by a hyperplane passing through $\mathbf{X}_N$.

We must now calculate $L_{\mathbf{x}_N}(N-1, d)$. We shall show that

$$L_{\mathbf{x}_N}(N-1, d) = L(N-1, d-1) \tag{2.32}$$

The argument used in verifying the above equation is as follows: First construct a line (one-dimensional hyperplane) through $\mathbf{X}_N$ and each point

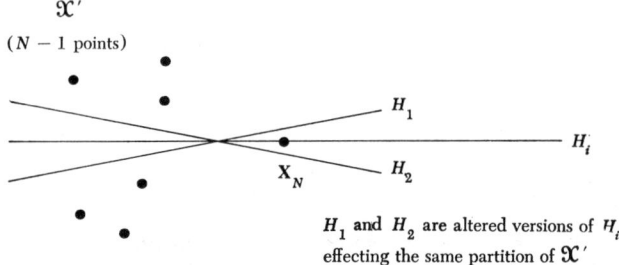

H_1 and H_2 are altered versions of H_i effecting the same partition of $\mathfrak{X}'$

FIGURE 2·10 Two separations of $\mathfrak{X}$ in E^2

in $\mathfrak{X}'$. We now have a set of $N-1$ lines. Because the members of $\mathfrak{X}$ are in general position, each of these lines is distinct (i.e., no three points of $\mathfrak{X}$ are on the same line). Select some hyperplane H having an intersection with each of these lines and let these intersections be given by the $N-1$ points in the set $\mathcal{P} = \{\mathbf{P}_1, \ldots, \mathbf{P}_{N-1}\}$. Clearly, the number of separations of $\mathfrak{X}$ by a $(d-1)$-dimensional hyperplane passing through $\mathbf{X}_N$ is equal to the number of separations of $\mathcal{P}$ by a $(d-2)$-dimensional hyperplane in H. But H is a $(d-1)$-dimensional space, and therefore the number of linear separations of $\mathcal{P}$ is equal to $L(N-1, d-1)$ thus verifying Eq. (2·32). The set $\mathcal{P}$ is in general position in a $(d-1)$-dimensional space as a consequence of the general position of $\mathfrak{X}$. Therefore, we can use the

---

* To illustrate, let H_i be a hyperplane which partitions $\mathfrak{X}'$ and suppose that H_i can be made to pass through $\mathbf{X}_N$ without altering the partition of $\mathfrak{X}'$. The hyperplane H_i can now be moved to one of two positions with respect to $\mathbf{X}_N$, still without altering the partition of $\mathfrak{X}'$. These positions are illustrated in Fig. 2·10 for the case $d = 2$.

SOME IMPORTANT DISCRIMINANT FUNCTIONS

recursion relation

$$L(N,d) = L(N-1, d) + L(N-1, d-1) \tag{2.33}$$

to solve for $L(N,d)$. Using the obvious boundary conditions

$$L(1,d) = 2 \quad \text{and} \quad L(N,1) = 2N \tag{2.34}$$

it is easy to verify that $L(N,d)$ is given by

$$L(N,d) = 2 \sum_{i=0}^{d} \binom{N-1}{i} \quad \text{for } N > d$$
$$= 2^N \quad \text{for } N \leq d \tag{2.35}$$

where $\binom{N-1}{i}$ is the binomial coefficient $(N-1)!/(N-1-i)!i!$.

The values of $L(N,d)$, for $N = 1$ through 8 and $d = 1$ through 5, are given in Table 2·2. The table can easily be extended to higher values of N and d by using the recursion equation (2·33).

TABLE 2·2 A partial table of $L(N,d)$

Number of patterns, N	Dimension, d				
	1	2	3	4	5
1	2	2	2	2	2
2	4	4	4	4	4
3	6	8	8	8	8
4	8	14	16	16	16
5	10	22	30	32	32
6	12	32	52	62	64
7	14	44	84	114	126
8	16	58	128	198	240

2·14 The effects of constraints

In the derivation of $L(N,d)$ we saw that the number of linear dichotomies of a set $\mathfrak{X}'$ of $N-1$ points, achievable by a hyperplane constrained to pass through a point $\mathbf{X}_N$, was equal to $L(N-1, d-1)$. That is, the effect of the single constraint on the separating hyperplane was to reduce

SOME IMPORTANT DISCRIMINANT FUNCTIONS

the dimension of the space by one. We shall generalize on this result in this section.

Suppose that we have a set $\mathfrak{X}$ of N points and a set $\mathfrak{Z}$ of K points ($K < d$) in E^d. We desire to know the number $L_\mathfrak{Z}(N,d)$ of linear dichotomies of $\mathfrak{X}$ achievable by a hyperplane constrained to contain all the points of $\mathfrak{Z}$. We shall assume that the points of $\mathfrak{Z}$ are in general position, meaning, in this case, that no $(K - 2)$-dimensional hyperplane contains all of them.

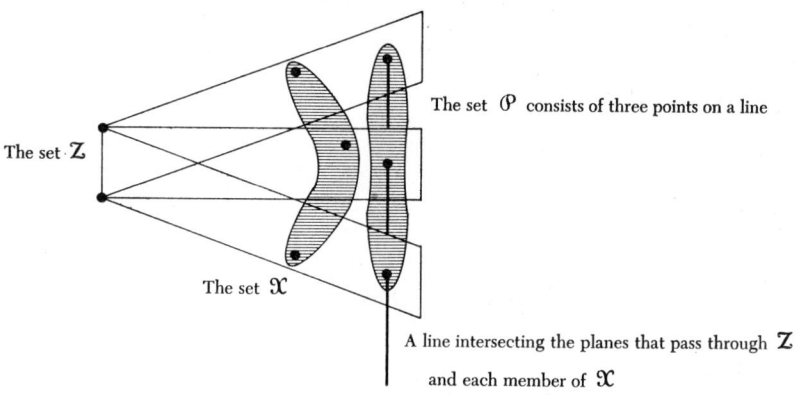

FIGURE 2·11 An illustration of the construction used in the text for $K = 2, N = 3, d = 3$

We now construct a set of N distinct K-dimensional hyperplanes, each containing $\mathfrak{Z}$ and one of the points in $\mathfrak{X}$. Figure 2·11 illustrates this construction. Let H be a $(d - K)$-dimensional hyperplane intersecting each of the N K-dimensional hyperplanes in a point. Let $\mathfrak{P}$ be the set of N intersection points. Clearly, the number of linear dichotomies of $\mathfrak{X}$ by $(d - 1)$-dimensional hyperplanes passing through $\mathfrak{Z}$ is equal to the number of linear dichotomies of $\mathfrak{P}$ by $(d - K - 1)$-dimensional hyperplanes in H.

We have an expression for this number if the points in $\mathfrak{P}$ are in general position on H. That is, no $(d - K + 1)$ or more of the points in $\mathfrak{P}$ can lie on the same $(d - K - 1)$-dimensional hyperplane. This condition is met if the points in $\mathfrak{X}$ satisfy the following (mild) conditions:

1. No $(d - K + 1)$ or more points of $\mathfrak{X}$ may lie on the same $(d - K - 1)$-dimensional hyperplane.
2. No $(d - K + 1)$ or more points of $\mathfrak{X}$ may lie on the same $(d - 1)$-dimensional hyperplane containing $\mathfrak{Z}$.

SOME IMPORTANT DISCRIMINANT FUNCTIONS

We see then that the effect of the K constraints imposed by $\mathcal{Z}$ is to reduce the dimensionality of the space by K. We then have

$$L_{\mathcal{Z}}(N,d) = L(N, d - K) \tag{2.36}$$

2·15 The number of Φ function dichotomies

Suppose our discriminant function family is of the form

$$g(\mathbf{X}) = w_1 f_1(\mathbf{X}) + \cdots + w_M f_M(\mathbf{X}) + w_{M+1} \tag{2.37}$$

that is, a Φ function family. We shall assume that the functions $f_i(\mathbf{X})$, $i = 1, \ldots, M$, are such that the loci of points in the pattern space satisfying the equations $g(\mathbf{X}) = 0$ are families of surfaces. The separations that these surfaces (called Φ surfaces) effect on a set $\mathcal{X}$ of N points are called Φ *dichotomies*. If there is no Φ surface in the pattern space containing $M + 1$ or more members of $\mathcal{X}$, then we say that the members of $\mathcal{X}$ are in Φ *general position*.

For any Φ function family, we desire to know the number $\Phi(N,d)$ of Φ dichotomies of a set $\mathcal{X}$ of N points in the pattern space. Corresponding to each point $\mathbf{X}$ in the pattern space there is a point $\mathbf{F} = \{f_1(\mathbf{X}), \ldots, f_M(\mathbf{X})\}$ in Φ space; therefore, corresponding to the set $\mathcal{X}$ of N points in Φ general position in the pattern space, there is a set $\mathcal{F}$ of N points in general position in the Φ space. Since any linear dichotomy of $\mathcal{F}$ in Φ space corresponds to a Φ dichotomy of $\mathcal{X}$ in the pattern space, $\Phi(N,d)$ is equal to $L(N,M)$, which is the number of linear dichotomies of the set $\mathcal{F}$ of N points in Φ space.

For the members of $\mathcal{X}$ in Φ general position we thus express the number of dichotomies of $\mathcal{X}$ implementable by *any* Φ function family as

$$\begin{aligned}\Phi(N,d) = L(N,M) &= 2 \sum_{i=0}^{M} \binom{N-1}{i} \quad \text{for } N > M \\ &= 2^N \quad \text{for } N \leq M\end{aligned} \tag{2.38}$$

The following special cases of Φ functions will illustrate the use of the above expression:

1. $\Phi(\mathbf{X})$ is a special quadric function of the form

$$\Phi(\mathbf{X}) = |\mathbf{X} - \mathbf{W}|^2 - a^2 \tag{2.39}$$

Here, $\Phi(\mathbf{X}) = 0$ defines a hypersphere, where $\mathbf{W}$ is the center of the hypersphere and a is its radius. Expanding the above equation yields

$$\Phi(\mathbf{X}) = \mathbf{X} \cdot \mathbf{X} - 2\mathbf{X} \cdot \mathbf{W} + \mathbf{W} \cdot \mathbf{W} - a^2 \tag{2.40}$$

Therefore $\mathbf{F}$ is $(d + 1)$-dimensional; i.e., $M = d + 1$. The first d components of $\mathbf{F}$ can be taken to be the d components of $\mathbf{X}$, and the $(d + 1)$th component of $\mathbf{F}$ is $|\mathbf{X}|^2$. Therefore, for a hypersphere

$$\Phi(N,d) = L(N, d + 1) \tag{2.41}$$

The above expression assumes, of course, that the points in $\mathfrak{X}$ are in Φ general position; that is, no $d + 2$ points in $\mathfrak{X}$ lie on the same hypersphere. We conclude that a hypersphere decision surface is slightly more powerful than a hyperplane decision surface, since $L(N, d + 1) > L(N,d)$ (see Table 2.2).

2. $\Phi(\mathbf{X})$ is an rth-order polynomial function. The function $f_i(\mathbf{X})$ is of the form $x_{k_1}{}^{n_1} x_{k_2}{}^{n_2} \ldots x_{k_r}{}^{n_r}$, $k_1, k_2, \ldots, k_r = 1, \ldots, d$; and $n_1, n_2, \ldots, n_r = 0$ and 1. In this case M is given by

$$M = \sum_{i=1}^{r} \binom{d + i - 1}{i} \\ = \binom{d + r}{r} - 1 \tag{2.42}$$

If $r = 2$ we have a general quadric function for which $M = d(d + 3)/2$, as derived in Sec. 2.10. For general quadric functions

$$\Phi(N,d) = L\left[N, \frac{d(d + 3)}{2}\right] \tag{2.43}$$

Note that the general quadric surface is a much more powerful decision surface than is the hyperplane or the hypersphere.

2·16 Machine capacity

Suppose that we are given a Φ machine with $M + 1$ adjustable weights and a set $\mathfrak{X}$ of N patterns in Φ general position in the pattern space. There are 2^N possible dichotomies of these patterns; if one of these dichotomies is selected at random (with probability 2^{-N}), what is the probability $P_{N,M}$ that it can be implemented (for some setting of the weights) by the given Φ machine? The answer is obtained by dividing the number of

Φ dichotomies by 2^N. That is,

$$P_{N,M} = 2^{1-N} \sum_{i=0}^{M} \binom{N-1}{i} \quad \text{for } N > M$$
$$= 1 \quad \text{for } N \leq M \quad (2\cdot 44)$$

The probability $P_{N,M}$ has a number of interesting characteristics. These can best be seen if we normalize by setting $N = \lambda(M + 1)$. A plot of the function $P_{\lambda(M+1),M}$ versus λ for various values of M appears in Fig. 2·12.

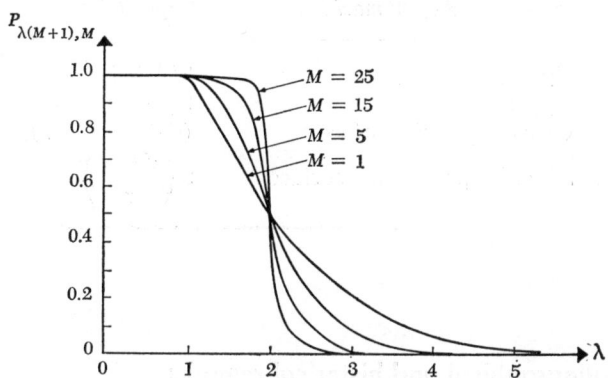

FIGURE 2·12 $P_{\lambda(M+1),M}$ versus λ for various values of M

Note the pronounced threshold effect, for large $M + 1$, around $\lambda = 2$. Also note that for each value of M

$$P_{2(M+1),M} = \tfrac{1}{2} \quad (2\cdot 45)$$

The threshold effect around $2(M + 1)$ can be expressed quantitively by

$$\lim_{M \to \infty} P_{(2+\epsilon)(M+1),M} = 0 \quad \text{for all } \epsilon > 0$$

and

$$\lim_{M \to \infty} P_{(2-\epsilon)(M+1),M} = 1 \quad \text{for all } \epsilon > 0 \quad (2\cdot 46)$$

These characteristics of $P_{N,M}$ lead us naturally to define the capacity C of a Φ machine as

$$C = 2(M + 1) \quad (2\cdot 47)$$

That is, the capacity is twice the number of degrees of freedom or twice the number of weights in the Φ machine. For large M we can be almost certain of being able to achieve any specific dichotomy of fewer than C

patterns with a given Φ machine. On the other hand, we are almost certain to fail to achieve any specific dichotomy of more than C patterns.

The capacity of a Φ machine is, then, a quite useful measure of its ability to dichotomize patterns.* To compare the various Φ machines that we have discussed in this chapter, we tabulate their capacities in Table 2·3.

TABLE 2 · 3   The capacities of some Φ machines

Decision boundary in pattern space implemented by Φ machine	Capacity
Hyperplane	$2(d + 1)$
Hypersphere	$2(d + 2)$
General quadric surface	$(d + 1)(d + 2)$
rth-order polynomial surface	$2\binom{d + r}{r}$

2 · 17   Bibliographical and historical remarks

A detailed treatment of the properties of hyperplane decision surfaces is contained in reports by Highleyman.[1,2] The *Learning Matrix* of Steinbuch[3] is an example of a trainable pattern-classifying machine with linear discriminant functions. The TLU and the subject of pairwise linear separability have been well studied by switching theorists; a paper by Winder[4] contains an excellent survey of the switching theory literature on the TLU. Tests for linear separability have been developed by Singleton[5] and others.

The implementation of a quadric machine (Fig. 2·8) was proposed by Koford.[6] The material on Φ functions is based on the work of Cover.[7,8]

Papers by Joseph,[9] Winder,[10] and Cameron[11] all contain calculations of the number of linear dichotomies of N d-dimensional points. The

* Our expression for the capacity of a Φ machine is based on the number of dichotomies it can implement. Generalization of this treatment for $R > 2$ leads to the question: How many of the R^N classifications of N patterns in d dimensions can a given Φ machine implement? We have seen that for $R = 2$ the answer to this question is independent of the position of the pattern points (provided that they are in general position). The answer for $R > 2$ has not yet been obtained and may not be independent of the position of the pattern points.

derivation of this number given in Sec. 2·13 is a version of one given by Cover.[7,8] The effects of constraints on the number of linear dichotomies and the extension of these results to Φ surfaces are also due to Cover.[7] Based on experimental and theoretical results on the number of linear dichotomies, both Koford[12] and Brown[13] suggested that the capacity of a TLU was equal to twice the number of variable weights. Winder[14] has also supported this conclusion. Further theoretical work by Cover and Efron[15] and later by Cover[7,8] provided the basis for the material on machine capacity in Sec. 2·16.

REFERENCES

1 Highleyman, W. H.: "Linear Decision Functions, with Applications to Pattern Recognition," Ph.D. Dissertation, Elect. Eng. Dept., Polytechnic Institute of Brooklyn, New York, June, 1961.
2 ———: Linear Decision Functions with Application to Pattern Recognition, *Proc. IRE*, vol. 50, no. 6, pp. 1501–1514, June, 1962.
3 Steinbuch, K., and V. A. W. Piske: Learning Matrices and Their Applications, *Trans. IEEE on Elect. Computers*, vol. EC-12, no. 5, pp. 846–862, December, 1963.
4 Winder, R. O.: Threshold Logic in Artificial Intelligence, *IEEE Publication S-142, Artificial Intelligence* (a combined preprint of papers presented at the winter general meeting, 1963), pp. 107–128, New York, 1963.
5 Singleton, R. C.: A Test for Linear Separability as Applied to Self-organizing Machines, in Yovits, Jacobi, and Goldstein (eds.), "Self-organizing Systems —1962," pp. 503–524, Spartan Books, Washington, D.C., 1962.
6 Koford, J.: Adaptive Network Organization, *Stanford Electronics Laboratory Quarterly Research Review No. 3*, III-6, 1962.
7 Cover, T. M.: Classification and Generalization Capabilities of Linear Threshold Units, *Rome Air Development Center Technical Documentary Report RADC-TDR*-64-32, February, 1964.
8 ———: Geometrical and Statistical Properties of Linear Threshold Devices, *Stanford Electronics Laboratories Technical Report* 6107-1, May, 1964.
9 Joseph, R. D.: The Number of Orthants in n-Space Intersected by an s-Dimensional Subspace, *Tech. Memorandum* 8, Project PARA, Cornell Aeronautical Laboratory, Buffalo, New York, 1960.
10 Winder, R. O.: "Threshold Logic," Ph.D. dissertation, Princeton University, Princeton, New Jersey, 1962.
11 Cameron, S. H.: An Estimate of the Complexity Requisite in a Universal Decision Network, "Proceedings of 1960 Bionics Symposium," *Wright Air Development Division Technical Report* 60-600, pp. 197–211, December, 1960.

SOME IMPORTANT DISCRIMINANT FUNCTIONS

12 Widrow, B.: Generalization and Information Storage in Networks of Adaline "Neurons," in Yovits, Jacobi, and Goldstein (eds.), "Self-organizing Systems—1962," p. 442, Spartan Books, Washington, D.C., 1962.
13 Brown, R.: Logical Properties of Adaptive Networks, *Stanford Electronics Laboratory Quarterly Research Review No. 4*, III-6–III-9, 1963.
14 Winder, R. O.: Bounds on Threshold Gate Realizability, *Trans. IEEE on Elect. Computers*, vol. EC-12, no. 5, pp. 561–564, October, 1963.
15 Cover, T. M., and B. Efron: paper in preparation.

CHAPTER 3

PARAMETRIC TRAINING METHODS

3 · 1 Probabilistic pattern sets

Having described some of the properties of various discriminant function families, we are now ready to discuss some training methods for selecting appropriate discriminant functions in the design of a pattern classifier. We shall begin by assuming that the pattern classes are characterized by sets of parameters (for example, cluster points). The values of these parameters might be unknown a priori. If the parameters were known, we assume that discriminant functions based on them could have been readily specified. Parametric training methods are those that use the set of training patterns to establish estimates of the values of the parameters; these estimates are then used for the specification of the discriminant functions.

An important situation in which the pattern classes are characterized by sets of parameters occurs when the patterns in each of the R categories are random variables governed by R distinct probability functions. Suppose we denote these probability functions by the symbol $p(\mathbf{X}|i)$,

$i = 1, \ldots, R$. Here, $p(\mathbf{X}|i)$ is the probability* of occurrence of pattern $\mathbf{X}$, given that it belongs to category i. We assume that the $p(\mathbf{X}|i)$ are known functions of a finite number of characteristic parameters whose values we might not know a priori. For example, we may know that the $p(\mathbf{X}|i)$, $i = 1, \ldots, R$, are normal probability-density functions with unknown means. An additional set of parameters, whose values might also be unknown, are the a priori probabilities for each class $p(i)$, $i = 1, \ldots, R$.

In such a probabilistic situation the set of patterns in each category is characterized by a parameter set: the number $p(i)$ and the parameters of the function $p(\mathbf{X}|i)$. The parametric training method for the design of discriminant functions then consists of three steps:

1. The discriminant functions are expressed in terms of the values of the parameters of the $p(\mathbf{X}|i)$ and of the parameters $p(i)$.
2. The values of the parameters of the $p(\mathbf{X}|i)$ and of the parameters $p(i)$ are estimated from a set of training patterns.
3. These estimates are then presumed to be the true values of the parameters and are used in the expressions for the discriminant functions developed in step 1.

There are some important problems in pattern classification in which these steps can be easily applied. This chapter is devoted to a study of the parametric training method as it is used in these problems.

3·2 Discriminant functions based on decision theory

Statistical decision theory can be used as a means to establish the discriminant functions for probabilistic patterns governed by known probability functions. Central to the decision-theoretic treatment is the specification of a *loss function*, $\lambda(i|j)$. Here $\lambda(i|j)$ is a function defined for $i = 1, \ldots, R$ and $j = 1, \ldots, R$ and represents the loss incurred when the machine places a pattern actually belonging to category j into category i. If a machine classifies patterns such that the average value of $\lambda(i|j)$ is minimized, the machine is said to be *optimum*.† Decision theory deals with methods of specifying optimum machines.

Suppose that we had a machine which, whenever a particular pattern $\mathbf{X}$ occurred, always decided that $\mathbf{X}$ belonged to category i. On each such

* If $\mathbf{X}$ can assume a continuum of values, we interpret $p(\mathbf{X}|i)$ as a probability-density function.

† It is also called a *Bayes* machine.

decision we would incur a loss of $\lambda(i|j)$, where j is the actual category of pattern **X**. The probability that, given **X**, its category is j is written $p(j|\mathbf{X})$. The value of the loss averaged over those instances when **X** occurs is called a *conditional average loss* and is denoted by the symbol $L_\mathbf{X}(i)$, which is expressed by

$$L_\mathbf{X}(i) = \sum_{j=1}^{R} \lambda(i|j) p(j|\mathbf{X}) \tag{3.1}$$

Using Eq. (3·1), we could calculate $L_\mathbf{X}(i)$ for any specific **X** and for all possible values of i ($i = 1, \ldots, R$). Suppose for some specific **X**, $L_\mathbf{X}(i)$ is a minimum for $i = i_0$. That is, $L_\mathbf{X}(i_0) \leq L_\mathbf{X}(i)$ for $i = 1, \ldots, R$. We would minimize the conditional average loss if the machine always assigned this **X** to category i_0.

Similarly, for all other patterns we could attempt to minimize the respective conditional average losses by making appropriate classifications. There are as many conditional average losses as there are patterns. If the machine classifies patterns in such a way that the loss for each is minimized, then the value of the conditional loss averaged over all possible patterns will also be minimized. Therefore, the optimum machine makes its classifications by the following steps:

1. The pattern, say **X**, is presented to the machine.
2. The machine calculates $L_\mathbf{X}(i)$ for $i = 1, \ldots, R$.
3. The machine decides that **X** belongs to that category i_0 for which $L_\mathbf{X}(i_0) \leq L_\mathbf{X}(i)$ for all $i = 1, \ldots, R$.

The above rule suggests an obvious set of discriminant functions, namely, the negatives of $L_\mathbf{X}(i)$. By some additional manipulations, however, and for a special form of loss function, we can obtain a set of equivalent, but simpler, discriminant functions. These simplifications are developed in the next two sections.

3·3 Likelihoods

By Bayes' rule we can write

$$p(j|\mathbf{X}) = \frac{p(\mathbf{X}|j) p(j)}{p(\mathbf{X})} \tag{3.2}$$

where $p(\mathbf{X}|j)$ is the probability that **X** occurs, given that it is a pattern belonging to category j; regarded as a function of j, $p(\mathbf{X}|j)$ is often called the *likelihood* of j with respect to **X**; $p(j)$ is the a priori probability of occurrence of category j; and $p(\mathbf{X})$ is the probability that $\mathbf{X}$ occurs (regardless of its category).

Substitution of Eq. (3·2) into Eq. (3·1) yields

$$L_{\mathbf{x}}(i) = \frac{1}{p(\mathbf{X})} \sum_{j=1}^{R} \lambda(i|j) p(\mathbf{X}|j) p(j) \qquad (3\cdot 3)$$

In the computation of the $L_{\mathbf{x}}(i)$ for $i = 1, \ldots, R$, note that the quantity $1/p(\mathbf{X})$ occurs as a common factor. Therefore, the value of i that minimizes $L_{\mathbf{x}}(i)$ for any given $\mathbf{X}$ also minimizes

$$l_{\mathbf{x}}(i) \triangleq \sum_{j=1}^{R} \lambda(i|j) p(\mathbf{X}|j) p(j) \qquad (3\cdot 4)$$

3·4 A special loss function

We have shown that an optimum classifying machine could be achieved by computing and comparing the $l_{\mathbf{x}}(i)$. The computations are particularly simple if the loss function $\lambda(i|j)$ is assumed to be of the type

$$\lambda(i|j) = 1 - \delta_{ij} \qquad (3\cdot 5)$$

where δ_{ij} is the Kronecker delta function having a value of unity when $i = j$ and a value of zero otherwise. That is, we assume that we lose one unit whenever an error in classification is made, but lose nothing for correct classifications. Such a loss function shall be called a *symmetrical loss function*.

Substitution of Eq. (3·5) into Eq. (3·4) yields

$$l_{\mathbf{x}}(i) = p(\mathbf{X}) - p(\mathbf{X}|i) p(i) \qquad (3\cdot 6)$$

The above expression can be minimized with respect to i by maximizing $p(\mathbf{X}|i) p(i)$. Deciding in favor of the maximizing i minimizes the average loss. It can be shown that this decision rule also minimizes the probability of erroneous classification. If all categories are equally likely a priori (that is, if $p(i) = 1/R$ for $i = 1, \ldots, R$), the machine need only compute $p(\mathbf{X}|i)$ for all $i = 1, \ldots, R$, and select the maximizing i. Such a decision is known as a *maximum-likelihood* decision.

For the symmetrical loss function, we can summarize as follows: A decision-theoretic approach leads to discriminant functions that can be simply expressed in terms of the probability functions $p(\mathbf{X}|i)$, $i = 1, \ldots, R$, and the a priori probabilities $p(i)$, $i = 1, \ldots, R$. Specifically, for this loss function, the discriminant functions can be expressed as

$$g_i(\mathbf{X}) = p(\mathbf{X}|i)p(i) \qquad \text{for } i = 1, \ldots, R \qquad (3 \cdot 7a)$$

It will often be convenient to use the alternative expression

$$g_i(\mathbf{X}) = \log p(\mathbf{X}|i) + \log p(i) \qquad \text{for } i = 1, \ldots, R \qquad (3 \cdot 7b)$$

which leads to the same decisions since the log function is a monotonic-increasing function of its argument.

3·5 An example

Suppose that we wish to design a machine to categorize patterns each consisting of d binary components. (Each $x_i = 1$ or 0.) Let us assume that $R = 2$; that is, there are two categories, labeled category 1 and category 2.

We shall carry out the steps involved in the specification of the discriminant functions for the optimum classifying machine to illustrate the use of the concepts developed above. We shall assume that $\lambda(i|j)$ is a symmetrical loss function; that is, $\lambda(1|1) = 0$, $\lambda(1|2) = 1$, $\lambda(2|1) = 1$, and $\lambda(2|2) = 0$. As in Chapter 1, we define the discriminant function, $g(\mathbf{X}) = g_1(\mathbf{X}) - g_2(\mathbf{X})$. If $g(\mathbf{X}) > 0$, the machine places $\mathbf{X}$ in category 1; if $g(\mathbf{X}) < 0$, the machine places $\mathbf{X}$ in category 2. From Eq. (3·7b) we can derive

$$g(\mathbf{X}) = \log\left[\frac{p(\mathbf{X}|1)}{p(\mathbf{X}|2)}\right] + \log\left[\frac{p(1)}{p(2)}\right] = \log\left[\frac{p(\mathbf{X}|1)}{p(\mathbf{X}|2)}\right] + \log\left[\frac{p(1)}{1 - p(1)}\right] \qquad (3 \cdot 8)$$

We assume that we know the *form* of the probability functions $p(\mathbf{X}|1)$ and $p(\mathbf{X}|2)$. Specifically, let us assume for this example that for both categories the components of $\mathbf{X}$ are statistically independent. This assumption allows us to write

$$p(\mathbf{X}|j) = p(x_1|j)p(x_2|j) \cdots p(x_d|j) \qquad j = 1, 2 \qquad (3 \cdot 9)$$

The $p(x_i|j)$ for $j = 1$ and 2 and $i = 1, \ldots, d$ are the parameters of the distributions $p(\mathbf{X}|j)$. Some or all of their values might be unknown. Thus we have a situation in which application of the parametric training method is appropriate.

Our first step is to derive simple expressions for the discriminant functions. Substitution of Eq. (3·9) into Eq. (3·8) yields

$$g(\mathbf{X}) = \sum_{i=1}^{d} \log\left[\frac{p(x_i|1)}{p(x_i|2)}\right] + \log\left[\frac{p(1)}{1 - p(1)}\right] \qquad (3 \cdot 10)$$

48 PARAMETRIC TRAINING METHODS

For economy of notation we define

$$\begin{aligned} p(x_i = 1|1) &\triangleq p_i \\ p(x_i = 0|1) &\triangleq 1 - p_i \\ p(x_i = 1|2) &\triangleq q_i \\ p(x_i = 0|2) &\triangleq 1 - q_i \qquad i = 1, \ldots, d \end{aligned} \qquad (3\cdot 11)$$

Since x_i can assume only the values of one or zero, we note that

$$\begin{aligned} \log\left[\frac{p(x_i|1)}{p(x_i|2)}\right] &= x_i \log\left(\frac{p_i}{q_i}\right) + (1 - x_i)\log\left(\frac{1 - p_i}{1 - q_i}\right) \\ &= x_i \log\left[\frac{p_i(1 - q_i)}{q_i(1 - p_i)}\right] + \log\left(\frac{1 - p_i}{1 - q_i}\right) \end{aligned} \qquad (3\cdot 12)$$

Substitution of Eq. (3·12) into Eq. (3·10) yields

$$g(\mathbf{X}) = \sum_{i=1}^{d} x_i \log\left[\frac{p_i(1 - q_i)}{q_i(1 - p_i)}\right] + \sum_{i=1}^{d} \log\left(\frac{1 - p_i}{1 - q_i}\right) + \log\left[\frac{p(1)}{1 - p(1)}\right] \qquad (3\cdot 13)$$

The reader will recognize that the optimum discriminant function is

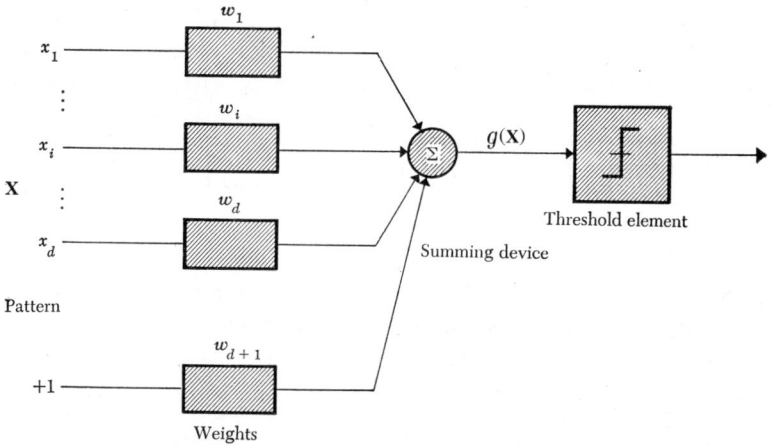

FIGURE 3·1 The optimum classifier for binary patterns whose components are statistically independent

linear in this case. Therefore a TLU can be used as the optimum classifying machine.* The block diagram of the TLU is given in Fig. 3·1. The weight

* There is an obvious generalization of this example for the case $R > 2$. The reader is invited to verify that the optimum classifying machine is still linear.

values are given by

$$w_i = \log\left[\frac{p_i(1-q_i)}{q_i(1-p_i)}\right] \quad i = 1, \ldots, d$$
$$w_{d+1} = \log\left[\frac{p(1)}{1-p(1)}\right] + \sum_{i=1}^{d} \log\left(\frac{1-p_i}{1-q_i}\right) \quad (3.14)$$

Investigation of Eqs. (3·13) and (3·14) in some limiting cases will show that the discriminant function depends in a reasonable way on the probabilities involved. Note, for example, that the values of the a priori probabilities $p(1)$ and $1 - p(1)$ affect only the value of w_{d+1}. As category 1 becomes less probable a priori, w_{d+1} decreases. Such a decrease of w_{d+1} favors a category 2 response for all patterns.

Note also that the ith weight w_i depends logarithmically on the ratio $(p_i/1 - p_i)/(q_i/1 - q_i)$. If p_i increases, with q_i constant, this ratio will also increase as will w_i. Such an increase of w_i favors a category-1 response for all patterns whose ith component is equal to one. The ith weight w_i will be equal to zero only when $p_i = q_i$, in which case the ith component of the pattern is properly ignored.

If we assume that some or all of the values of the p_i, the q_i, and $p(1)$ are unknown, the next step in the parametric training procedure consists in examining typical patterns to make estimates for the unknown values of the p_i, q_i, and $p(1)$. We then presume that these estimates are the true values and use them in Eq. (3·14) to specify the discriminant function.

Suppose that a number N of *typical* patterns have been examined, and that N_1 of them belong to category 1 and N_2 of them to category 2. Thus, $N_1 + N_2 = N$. Reasonable* estimates for the unknown probabili-

---

* The reader with background in statistics will recall that there are circumstances in which it is possible to make *optimum* estimates of unknown probability values. These optimum estimates are meaningful, however, only when the unknown probability values are themselves random variables with *known* probability distributions. As an example, consider the case of N successive Bernoulli trials where the probability of success is some number p. We assume that the value of p is unknown, but that it is governed by a uniform probability distribution over the interval zero to one. If the number of successes in N trials is n, then the estimate for p which minimizes the mean square error is given by $(n+1)/(N+2)$. Comparing this expression with those of Eq. (3·15) might lead the reader to assume that the estimates for the p_i and q_i could be improved by a slight modification. However, in view of the fact that neither the estimates given in Eq. (3·15) nor the modified estimates would be very reliable for a small sample size, and because the suggested modification is really no modification at all for a large sample size, it is probably pointless to debate which of these estimates should be used in the face of no a priori information about p_i and q_i.

50 PARAMETRIC TRAINING METHODS

ties might then be:

$$p_i = \frac{\text{number of typical patterns belonging to category 1 for which the } i\text{th component equals one}}{N_1}$$

$$q_i = \frac{\text{number of typical patterns belonging to category 2 for which the } i\text{th component equals one}}{N_2}$$

$$p(1) = \frac{N_1}{N} \qquad (3\cdot 15)$$

These estimates could then be used in Eq. (3·14) to establish values of the TLU weights and threshold.

3·6 The bivariate normal probability-density function

In the example of Sec. 3·5, we assumed that the pattern components were statistically independent, binary, random variables. Such an assumption permitted a straightforward calculation of the discriminant function for the optimum classifying machine. The optimum classifier can also be readily derived when the pattern components are normally distributed random variables. The normal or Gaussian probability-density function is important because of its computational simplicity and because it represents a realistic model of many pattern-classification situations. Furthermore, normal distributions encompass some situations in which the individual pattern components are not statistically independent. In the following sections we will review briefly some of the properties of the multivariate normal probability-density function. We shall begin by considering the *bivariate* normal density function.

The bivariate density function is a joint probability-density function of two random variables. Consider the two random variables x_1 and x_2. Let the mean values of x_1 and x_2 be equal to m_1 and m_2, respectively. Let the variances of x_1 and x_2 be equal to σ_{11} and σ_{22}, respectively.* Using $E[\ ]$ to denote the expectation operator, we then have

$$\begin{aligned} E[x_1] &= m_1 \\ E[x_2] &= m_2 \\ E[x_1{}^2] - E^2[x_1] &= \sigma_{11} \\ E[x_2{}^2] - E^2[x_2] &= \sigma_{22} \end{aligned} \qquad (3\cdot 16)$$

---

* Note that there is a departure here from conventional notation, in that σ_{11} is the *variance* of x_1, not the standard deviation.

PARAMETRIC TRAINING METHODS   51

In discussing the bivariate normal density function, it is convenient to consider the normalized and translated variables z_1 and z_2 defined by

$$z_1 = \frac{x_1 - m_1}{\sqrt{\sigma_{11}}}$$
$$z_2 = \frac{x_1 - m_2}{\sqrt{\sigma_{22}}} \qquad (3 \cdot 17)$$

Each of the new variables has a mean value equal to zero and a variance equal to unity.

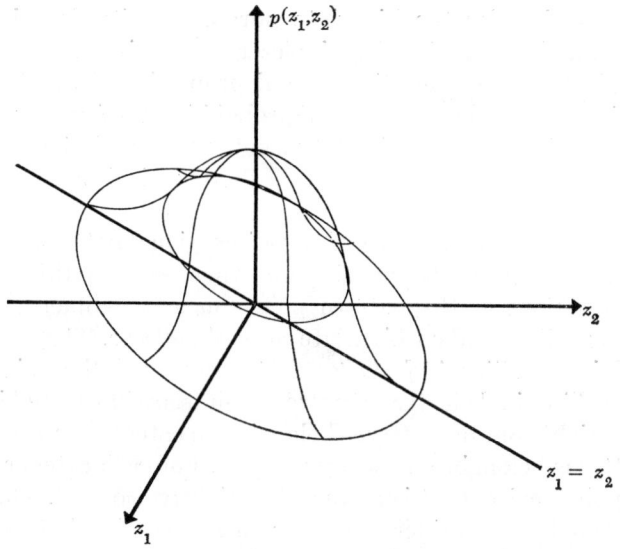

FIGURE 3·2   The bivariate normal density function

In terms of these normalized variables the bivariate normal density function is expressed by

$$p(z_1, z_2) = \frac{1}{2\pi \sqrt{1 - \sigma_{12}{}^2}} \exp\left\{ -\frac{1}{2} \frac{z_1{}^2 - 2\sigma_{12} z_1 z_2 + z_2{}^2}{1 - \sigma_{12}{}^2} \right\} \qquad (3 \cdot 18)$$

where σ_{12}, which is called the covariance or correlation of z_1 and z_2, is given by

$$\sigma_{12} = E[z_1 z_2] \qquad (3 \cdot 19)$$

It is a straightforward matter to show that $\sigma_{12}{}^2 \leq 1.$*

The function $p(z_1, z_2)$, plotted as a surface above the z_1, z_2 plane, is illustrated in Fig. 3·2. Note that $p(z_1, z_2)$ attains its maximum value at the

* The special case $\sigma_{12}{}^2 = 1$ corresponds to a degenerate situation in which z_2 is always equal to $\pm z_1$. Such a degeneracy indicates that the proper density function would be univariate rather than bivariate. We shall therefore always assume that $\sigma_{12}{}^2 < 1$.

origin and falls toward zero away from the origin. Contours of equal probability density ($z_1^2 - 2\sigma_{12}z_1z_2 + z_2^2 =$ constant) are ellipses, centered on the origin, whose major axes lie along the line $z_1 = z_2$. The eccentricities of the ellipses are equal to

$$\sqrt{\frac{2|\sigma_{12}|}{1 + |\sigma_{12}|}}$$

When σ_{12} is zero, the contours of equal probability are circles (zero eccentricity).

The expression for the bivariate normal density function for the unnormalized and untranslated variables x_1 and x_2 is more complicated* than that of Eq. (3·18), but the general properties of the function are easily described. The contours of equal probability density are still ellipses, and the picture is much like Fig. 3·2 except for a translation and stretching of the z_1 and z_2 axes. In general, the elliptical cross sections are centered at $x_1 = m_1$, $x_2 = m_2$.

Let us assume that a number of two-dimensional patterns are selected from a bivariate normal distribution and then see how this assumption affects the positions of the pattern points in a two-dimensional space. Such patterns will be called bivariate *normal patterns*. They will tend to be grouped in an *ellipsoidal cluster* centered around the point (m_1,m_2). Several such ellipsoidal clusters of pattern points are illustrated in Fig. 3·3. One cluster might contain patterns belonging to category 1; another might contain patterns belonging to category 2, etc. For each category a cluster of pattern points exists that is more or less tightly grouped. The center of each cluster could be considered a *prototype* pattern for that category. As the number of sample points in a cluster increases, the coordinates of the

---

* The general expression for the bivariate normal density function of x_1 and x_2 is

$$p(x_1,x_2) = \frac{1}{2\pi\sqrt{\sigma_{11}\sigma_{22} - \sigma_{12}^2}}$$

$$\exp\left\{-\frac{1}{2}\frac{\dfrac{(x_1 - m_1)^2}{\sigma_{11}} - \dfrac{2\sigma_{12}(x_1 - m_1)(x_2 - m_2)}{\sqrt{\sigma_{11}\sigma_{22}}} + \dfrac{(x_2 - m_2)^2}{\sigma_{22}}}{1 - \dfrac{\sigma_{12}^2}{\sigma_{11}\sigma_{22}}}\right\} \quad (3\cdot 20)$$

The covariance and variance terms are now given by

$$\sigma_{ij} = E[(x_i - m_i)(x_j - m_j)] \qquad i, j = 1, 2$$

The reader should verify that these definitions of the covariance and variance are consistent with those of Eqs. (3·16) and (3·19); the definition of Eq. (3·19) applied only to zero-mean random variables. The assumption made in the previous footnote should now be generalized to $\sigma_{12}^2 < \sigma_{11}\sigma_{22}$.

center of gravity of the cluster approach the mean values m_1, m_2 of the corresponding normal distribution.

The notation used in Eq. (3·20) to describe the normal distribution can be made more compact if we define and use the following matrices. Let the pattern vector **X** be a column vector (a 2×1 matrix) with compo-

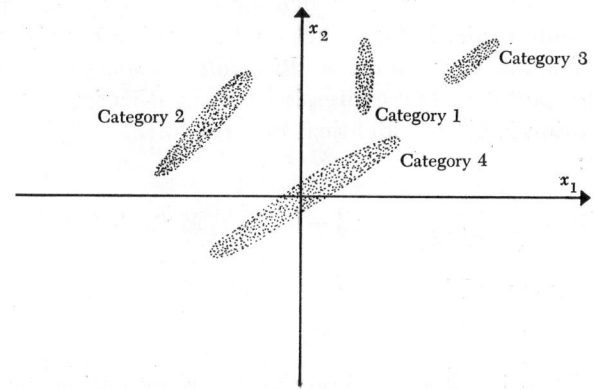

FIGURE 3·3 Ellipsoidal clusters of patterns

nents x_1 and x_2. Similarly, let the *mean vector* **M** be a column vector with components m_1 and m_2. We also define a 2×2 *covariance matrix*

$$\mathbf{\Sigma} = \begin{bmatrix} \sigma_{11} & \sigma_{12} \\ \sigma_{21} & \sigma_{22} \end{bmatrix}$$

where

$$\sigma_{21} = \sigma_{12}$$

In terms of these definitions we can rewrite Eq. (3·20) in the form

$$p(\mathbf{X}) = \frac{1}{2\pi |\mathbf{\Sigma}|^{1/2}} \exp\{-\tfrac{1}{2}(\mathbf{X} - \mathbf{M})^t \mathbf{\Sigma}^{-1}(\mathbf{X} - \mathbf{M})\} \qquad (3\cdot 21)$$

where $(\mathbf{X} - \mathbf{M})^t$ is the transpose (row-vector form) of $(\mathbf{X} - \mathbf{M})$, $\mathbf{\Sigma}^{-1}$ is the inverse* of the matrix $\mathbf{\Sigma}$, and $|\mathbf{\Sigma}|$ is the determinant of $\mathbf{\Sigma}$.

$$\mathbf{\Sigma}^{-1} = \frac{1}{\sigma_{11}\sigma_{22} - \sigma_{12}^2} \begin{bmatrix} \sigma_{22} & -\sigma_{12} \\ -\sigma_{21} & \sigma_{11} \end{bmatrix} \qquad (3\cdot 22)$$

and

$$|\mathbf{\Sigma}| = \sigma_{11}\sigma_{22} - \sigma_{12}^2 \qquad (3\cdot 23)$$

The reader should verify that Eqs. (3·21) and (3·20) are identical.

* The matrix $\mathbf{\Sigma}$ is nonsingular as a consequence of the assumption that $\sigma_{12}^2 < \sigma_{11}\sigma_{22}$.

3·7 The multivariate normal distribution

The matrix notation of the last section has a direct parallel in the case in which the number of pattern components is greater than two. There is a *multivariate normal distribution* which describes the joint probability density of d components. Patterns selected according to this joint probability distribution will be called *multivariate normal* patterns or, more simply, *normal patterns*. The expression for the d-variate normal probability distribution is almost identical in form to that of Eq. (3·21). It is the following:

$$p(\mathbf{X}) = \frac{1}{(2\pi)^{d/2}|\mathbf{\Sigma}|^{1/2}} \exp\{-\tfrac{1}{2}(\mathbf{X} - \mathbf{M})^t \mathbf{\Sigma}^{-1}(\mathbf{X} - \mathbf{M})\} \qquad (3\cdot24)$$

The various terms used in Eq. (3·24) are defined below.

$\mathbf{X} = \begin{pmatrix} x_1 \\ x_2 \\ \ldots \\ x_d \end{pmatrix}$ is a $d \times 1$ column vector representing the pattern.

$\mathbf{M} = \begin{pmatrix} m_1 \\ m_2 \\ \ldots \\ m_d \end{pmatrix}$ is a $d \times 1$ column vector. It has the property of being equal to the expected value of $\mathbf{X}$ (i.e., $\mathbf{M} = E[\mathbf{X}]$) and is therefore called the *mean vector*.

$\mathbf{\Sigma} = \begin{bmatrix} \sigma_{11} & \sigma_{12} & \cdots & \sigma_{1d} \\ \cdots & \cdots & \sigma_{ij} & \cdots \\ \sigma_{d1} & & \cdots & \sigma_{dd} \end{bmatrix}$ is a symmetric, positive definite matrix, called the *covariance matrix*.

The i, j component σ_{ij} of the covariance matrix $\mathbf{\Sigma}$ is given by

$$\sigma_{ij} = E[(x_i - m_i)(x_j - m_j)] \qquad (3\cdot25)$$

for all $i, j = 1, \ldots, d$; in particular, σ_{ii} is the variance of x_i. We can also write $\mathbf{\Sigma}$ in the compact form

$$\mathbf{\Sigma} = E[(\mathbf{X} - \mathbf{M})(\mathbf{X} - \mathbf{M})^t] \qquad (3\cdot26)$$

The inverse of $\mathbf{\Sigma}$ is $\mathbf{\Sigma}^{-1}$, and the determinant of $\mathbf{\Sigma}$ is $|\mathbf{\Sigma}|$. Since the d-variate normal probability distribution is completely specified by the mean vector $\mathbf{M}$ and covariance matrix $\mathbf{\Sigma}$, we shall sometimes use the abbreviated notation

$$p(\mathbf{X}) \sim N(\mathbf{M}, \mathbf{\Sigma}) \qquad (3\cdot27)$$

The expression $(\mathbf{X} - \mathbf{M})^t \mathbf{\Sigma}^{-1}(\mathbf{X} - \mathbf{M})$ in the exponent of Eq. (3·24) is a positive definite quadratic form. The surfaces defined by setting this quadratic form equal to constants are hyperellipsoids centered on the point **M**. These ellipsoids are surfaces of equal probability in the d-dimensional pattern space. A set of normal patterns would then tend to be grouped in an ellipsoidal cluster centered around a prototype pattern **M**.

3·8 The optimum classifier for normal patterns

We are now ready to derive the optimum classifier for normal patterns. We shall temporarily assume that for each category i, where $i = 1, \ldots, R$, we know the a priori probability $p(i)$ and the particular d-variate normal probability function $p(\mathbf{X}|i)$ that apply. That is, we know R normal density functions, differing perhaps in their mean vectors and covariance matrices, and we know R numbers $p(i)$ for $i = 1, \ldots, R$.

Defining R mean vectors $\mathbf{M}_i$ for $i = 1, \ldots, R$, and R covariance matrices $\mathbf{\Sigma}_i$ for $i = 1, \ldots, R$, we write

$$p(\mathbf{X}|i) = \frac{1}{(2\pi)^{d/2}|\mathbf{\Sigma}_i|^{1/2}} \exp\{-\tfrac{1}{2}(\mathbf{X} - \mathbf{M}_i)^t \mathbf{\Sigma}_i^{-1}(\mathbf{X} - \mathbf{M}_i)\}$$
$$\text{for } i = 1, \ldots, R \quad (3.28)$$

We shall also adopt the convention $p(i) = p_i$.

In Sec. 3·4 we learned that for a symmetric loss function, the optimum classifier uses the discriminant functions given by

$$g_i(\mathbf{X}) = \log p(\mathbf{X}|i) + \log p_i \qquad i = 1, \ldots, R \quad (3.29)$$

Using Eq. (3·28), the $g_i(\mathbf{X})$ are given as follows:

$$g_i(\mathbf{X}) = \log p_i - \frac{d}{2}\log 2\pi - \tfrac{1}{2}\log|\mathbf{\Sigma}_i| - \tfrac{1}{2}[(\mathbf{X} - \mathbf{M}_i)^t \mathbf{\Sigma}_i^{-1}(\mathbf{X} - \mathbf{M}_i)]$$
$$i = 1, \ldots, R \quad (3.30)$$

Because the term $d/2 \log 2\pi$ is the same for all $i = 1, \ldots, R$, it can be disregarded. The expression $\log p_i - \tfrac{1}{2}\log|\mathbf{\Sigma}_i|$ does not depend on the particular pattern being classified, and it can therefore be thought of as a constant, denoted by b_i. Redefining $g_i(\mathbf{X})$ to exclude $-d/2 \log 2\pi$, we have

$$g_i(\mathbf{X}) = b_i - \tfrac{1}{2}[(\mathbf{X} - \mathbf{M}_i)^t \mathbf{\Sigma}_i^{-1}(\mathbf{X} - \mathbf{M}_i)] \qquad i = 1, \ldots, R \quad (3.31)$$

where

$$b_i = \log p_i - \tfrac{1}{2}\log|\mathbf{\Sigma}_i|$$

Thus, we see that the optimum discriminant functions for normal patterns are quadric functions.

3·9 Some special cases involving identical covariance matrices

For the optimum discriminant functions for normal patterns, expansion of Eq. (3·31) yields

$$g_i(\mathbf{X}) = -\tfrac{1}{2}\mathbf{X}^t\mathbf{\Sigma}_i^{-1}\mathbf{X} + \mathbf{X}^t\mathbf{\Sigma}_i^{-1}\mathbf{M}_i$$
$$- \tfrac{1}{2}\mathbf{M}_i^t\mathbf{\Sigma}_i^{-1}\mathbf{M}_i + \log p_i - \tfrac{1}{2}\log|\mathbf{\Sigma}_i| \qquad i = 1, \ldots, R \quad (3\cdot32)$$

In the special case in which it is known that all of the covariance matrices $\mathbf{\Sigma}_i$ (for $i = 1, \ldots, R$) are identical,* the terms $-\tfrac{1}{2}\mathbf{X}^t\mathbf{\Sigma}_i^{-1}\mathbf{X}$ and $-\tfrac{1}{2}\log|\mathbf{\Sigma}_i|$ can be omitted because they do not depend on the value of i. The discriminant functions can then be redefined to exclude these terms, yielding

$$g_i(\mathbf{X}) = \mathbf{X}^t\mathbf{\Sigma}^{-1}\mathbf{M}_i + \log p_i - \tfrac{1}{2}\mathbf{M}_i^t\mathbf{\Sigma}^{-1}\mathbf{M}_i \qquad (3\cdot33)$$

where $\mathbf{\Sigma}$ is the covariance matrix of each pattern class. We see that this case leads to linear discriminant functions and thus to linear machines. The first d weights employed by the ith discriminator are given by the values of the components of the transformed mean vector, $\mathbf{\Sigma}^{-1}\mathbf{M}_i$; the $(d + 1)$th weight is given by the value of the constant,

$$\log p_i - \tfrac{1}{2}\mathbf{M}_i^t\mathbf{\Sigma}^{-1}\mathbf{M}_i$$

If $R = 2$, and if $\mathbf{\Sigma}_1 = \mathbf{\Sigma}_2 = \mathbf{\Sigma}$, then the single discriminant function $g(\mathbf{X})$ can be written as

$$g(\mathbf{X}) = \mathbf{X}^t\mathbf{\Sigma}^{-1}(\mathbf{M}_1 - \mathbf{M}_2) - \tfrac{1}{2}\mathbf{M}_1^t\mathbf{\Sigma}^{-1}\mathbf{M}_1 + \tfrac{1}{2}\mathbf{M}_2^t\mathbf{\Sigma}^{-1}\mathbf{M}_2 + \log\left(\frac{p_1}{p_2}\right)$$
$$(3.34)$$

The hyperplane decision boundary given by $g(\mathbf{X}) = 0$ is normal to the line segment connecting the transformed means $\mathbf{\Sigma}^{-1}\mathbf{M}_1$ and $\mathbf{\Sigma}^{-1}\mathbf{M}_2$. Its

---

* For example, the covariance matrices describing the statistics of the pattern categories would be identical in the following often-discussed situation. Each pattern belonging to the ith category is a random vector given by the sum of a fixed, nonrandom vector $\mathbf{P}_i$ plus a random "noise" vector $\mathbf{N}_i$. The random vectors $\mathbf{N}_i$ ($i = 1, \ldots, R$) are drawn from the same normal distribution. This formulation has been thoroughly treated in the problem of signal identification over a noisy (Gaussian) channel.[7]

PARAMETRIC TRAINING METHODS

point of intersection with this line segment depends on the constant term

$$-\tfrac{1}{2}\mathbf{M}_1{}^t\mathbf{\Sigma}^{-1}\mathbf{M}_1 + \tfrac{1}{2}\mathbf{M}_2{}^t\mathbf{\Sigma}^{-1}\mathbf{M}_2 + \log\left(\frac{p_1}{p_2}\right)$$

As a further specialization, consider the case in which $\mathbf{\Sigma} = \mathbf{I}$ the identity matrix (or any scalar matrix), and $p_i = 1/R$ for $i = 1, \ldots, R$. That is, each set of patterns belonging to a single category is a hyperspherical cluster and each category is a priori equally probable. Then Eq. (3·33) could be written as

$$g_i(\mathbf{X}) = \mathbf{X} \cdot \mathbf{M}_i - \tfrac{1}{2}\mathbf{M}_i \cdot \mathbf{M}_i \qquad i = 1, \ldots, R \qquad (3\cdot35)$$

In Eq. (3·35) we have used the notation $\mathbf{X} \cdot \mathbf{M}_i$ rather than the equivalent $\mathbf{X}^t\mathbf{M}_i$ to hasten the reader's recognition of this set of discriminant functions. This set is the same as that used for the minimum-distance classifier with respect to points, which was discussed in Chapter 2 [cf. Eq. (2·5)]. The prototype points are the mean vectors $\mathbf{M}_1, \mathbf{M}_2, \ldots, \mathbf{M}_R$. When $R = 2$, the hyperplane decision surface bisects and is normal to the line segment joining $\mathbf{M}_1$ and $\mathbf{M}_2$.

3·10 Training with normal pattern sets

The *form* of the optimum classifying machine for normal patterns, a quadric machine, does not depend on the *values* of the parameters of the individual probability distributions; rather, it depends only on the *form* of the distributions. Even if the parameter values of the distributions, the $\mathbf{\Sigma}_i$ and $\mathbf{M}_i$, are not presently known, the optimum classifier can still be designed and constructed from the knowledge that the $p(\mathbf{X}|i)$ are normal. If the values of the weights in the quadric machine are adjustable they can be properly set whenever information about the $\mathbf{\Sigma}_i$ and $\mathbf{M}_i$ becomes available.

Suppose that a training set of typical patterns belonging to each of the R categories is available. It consists of R subsets denoted by $\mathfrak{X}_1, \mathfrak{X}_2, \ldots, \mathfrak{X}_R$, where $\mathfrak{X}_i$ is the training subset of all patterns belonging to category i. These subsets can be used to estimate $\mathbf{\Sigma}_i$ and $\mathbf{M}_i$.

For each set $\mathfrak{X}_i$, $i = 1, \ldots, R$, we define the sample statistics

$$\begin{aligned}\langle \mathbf{X} \rangle_i &= \frac{1}{N_i} \sum_{\mathbf{X} \in \mathfrak{X}_i} \mathbf{X} \\ \langle \mathbf{\Sigma} \rangle_i &= \frac{1}{N_i} \sum_{\mathbf{X} \in \mathfrak{X}_i} (\mathbf{X} - \langle \mathbf{X} \rangle_i)(\mathbf{X} - \langle \mathbf{X} \rangle_i)^t\end{aligned} \qquad (3\cdot36)$$

where N_i is the number of patterns in the training subset $\mathfrak{X}_i$; $\langle \mathbf{X} \rangle_i$ is called the sample mean (or center of gravity) of the ith category, and $\langle \mathbf{\Sigma} \rangle_i$ is called the sample covariance matrix of the ith category. The $\langle \mathbf{X} \rangle_i$ and $\langle \mathbf{\Sigma} \rangle_i$ are reasonable* estimates of $\mathbf{M}_i$ and $\mathbf{\Sigma}_i$, respectively. The use of these estimates to specify the discriminant functions would constitute a parametric training method.

An expression that is somewhat simpler than the one in Eq. (3·36) can be given for the sample covariance matrix. The first step in its development is to form a matrix $\mathbf{Q}_i$ whose columns are derived from the patterns in $\mathfrak{X}_i$. Subtract from each of the N_i patterns in $\mathfrak{X}_i$ the sample-mean pattern $\langle \mathbf{X} \rangle_i$; $\mathbf{Q}_i$ is then a $d \times N_i$ matrix whose N_i columns are these diminished sample patterns.

It is a straightforward matter to verify that the sample covariance matrix is proportional to the product of $\mathbf{Q}_i$ and its transpose. Specifically

$$\langle \mathbf{\Sigma} \rangle_i = \frac{1}{N_i} \mathbf{Q}_i \mathbf{Q}_i^t \qquad (3 \cdot 37)$$

We have always assumed in the preceding development that the covariance matrix $\mathbf{\Sigma}_i$ is nonsingular and therefore possesses an inverse. We shall show that if $\mathbf{\Sigma}_i$ is nonsingular, then so also (with probability one) will be the estimate of $\mathbf{\Sigma}_i$, $\langle \mathbf{\Sigma} \rangle_i$, if $N_i \geq d$. If $\langle \mathbf{\Sigma} \rangle_i$ were singular it would not possess an inverse as needed for the specification of the optimum classifier.

For $\langle \mathbf{\Sigma} \rangle_i$ to be nonsingular, its rank must be equal to d. Since $\langle \mathbf{\Sigma} \rangle_i$ has rank equal to rank $\mathbf{Q}_i \mathbf{Q}_i^t$, which is equal to rank $\mathbf{Q}_i$, and since rank $\mathbf{Q}_i \leq \min(d, N_i)$, rank $\langle \mathbf{\Sigma} \rangle_i < d$ if $N_i < d$. If $N_i \geq d$, $\mathbf{Q}_i$ will have rank equal to d if and only if there are no linear dependencies among the rows of $\mathbf{Q}_i$. Or, alternatively, $\mathbf{Q}_i$ is of rank d if and only if $\mathbf{Q}_i$ contains at least d linearly independent columns. These requirements can be interpreted as the geometrical requirement that not all the pattern vectors in $\mathfrak{X}_i$ may lie on the same $(d-1)$-dimensional hyperplane passing through the origin [a $(d-1)$-dimensional subspace]. If the unknown $\mathbf{\Sigma}_i$ itself is nonsingular, then the probability that $\mathfrak{X}_i$ lies in a subspace is zero. Therefore, for $N_i > d$ and for $\mathbf{\Sigma}_i$ nonsingular, we are assured that $\langle \mathbf{\Sigma} \rangle_i$ will be nonsingular.

3·11 Learning the mean vector of normal patterns

We have suggested that parametric training for a normal pattern classifier be accomplished by using the sample means and covariance matrices

* Unless we assume certain probability distributions for $\mathbf{M}_i$ and $\mathbf{\Sigma}_i$ it is meaningless to speak of *optimum* estimates.

derived from the training set as if they were the known means and covariance matrices. If we assume appropriate probability distributions for the unknown mean vectors and covariance matrices, we can derive a training process which makes optimum use of the set of training patterns. In this section we shall illustrate this derivation for the case in which the covariance matrices are all known but for which the mean vectors are assumed to be random variables.

Suppose the pattern vectors belonging to category i are normal with *known* covariance matrix Σ_i and unknown mean vector. Thus, the d components of the mean vector are the only unknown parameters of the discriminant function. For any known $\mathbf{M}$, $\mathbf{X}$ will be normal with mean $\mathbf{M}$ and covariance matrix Σ.* That is,

$$p(\mathbf{X}|\mathbf{M}) \sim N(\mathbf{M},\Sigma) \qquad (3 \cdot 38)$$

Suppose we assume that $\mathbf{M}$ is a normal vector with mean $\mathbf{\mu}$, and covariance matrix $\mathbf{K}$. That is,

$$p(\mathbf{M}) \sim N(\mathbf{\mu},\mathbf{K}) \qquad (3 \cdot 39)$$

Here, $\mathbf{\mu}$ is a priori the most probable value of the unknown mean vector, and $\mathbf{K}$ is a measure of its uncertainty.

We now want to compute the unconditional density function for $\mathbf{X}$. This task is made simpler by observing that $\mathbf{X}$ can be regarded as the sum of $\mathbf{M}$ and another independent normal vector $\mathbf{Z}$; that is,

$$\mathbf{X} = \mathbf{Z} + \mathbf{M} \qquad (3 \cdot 40)$$

The vector $\mathbf{Z}$ has zero mean and covariance matrix Σ. The conditional density for $\mathbf{X}$, given $\mathbf{M}$, is still given by Eq. (3·38). The unconditional density for $\mathbf{X}$ can now be obtained by inspection, since $\mathbf{Z}$ and $\mathbf{M}$ are independent. Then $\mathbf{X}$ will have mean $\mathbf{\mu}$ and covariance matrix $\Sigma + \mathbf{K}$. That is,

$$p(\mathbf{X}) \sim N(\mathbf{\mu}, \Sigma + \mathbf{K}) \qquad (3 \cdot 41)$$

The net effect of the uncertainty in $\mathbf{M}$ is to increase the covariance matrix of $\mathbf{X}$ from Σ to $\Sigma + \mathbf{K}$. Equation (3·31) with $\mathbf{M}$ replaced by $\mathbf{\mu}$ and Σ replaced by $\Sigma + \mathbf{K}$ gives the optimum a priori (before training) discriminant function.

The value of the present probabilistic model is that the unconditional density function for $\mathbf{X}$ changes as a result of being given a set of training patterns. We can see how it changes by first calculating an a posteriori density function for the mean vector $\mathbf{M}$. (By an *a posteriori density function* we mean the density function conditioned on knowing the training set.)

Suppose that the training subset (of the ith category) consists of the single vector $\mathbf{X}_1$. We shall show that the a posteriori density function for

---

* We simplify the ensuing discussion by dropping the subscript i.

M is normal; that is,
$$p(\mathbf{M}|\mathbf{X}_1) \sim N(\mathbf{\mu}_1, \mathbf{K}_1) \tag{3.42}$$

where expressions for $\mathbf{\mu}_1$ and $\mathbf{K}_1$ will be derived shortly. This a posteriori distribution for **M** implies that

$$p(\mathbf{X}|\mathbf{X}_1) \sim N(\mathbf{\mu}_1, \mathbf{\Sigma} + \mathbf{K}_1) \tag{3.43}$$

That is, the single training vector has changed the mean of **X** from $\mathbf{\mu}$ to $\mathbf{\mu}_1$, and the covariance matrix from $\mathbf{\Sigma} + \mathbf{K}$ to $\mathbf{\Sigma} + \mathbf{K}_1$. Training the classifying machine on the pattern $\mathbf{X}_1$ is accomplished by modifying the discriminant functions in accordance with these changes in the mean and covariance matrix for **X**.

The derivation of $\mathbf{\mu}_1$ and $\mathbf{K}_1$ proceeds as follows: By Bayes' rule we have

$$p(\mathbf{M}|\mathbf{X}_1) = \frac{p(\mathbf{X}_1|\mathbf{M})p(\mathbf{M})}{p(\mathbf{X}_1)} \tag{3.44}$$

But

$$p(\mathbf{X}_1|\mathbf{M}) \sim N(\mathbf{M}, \mathbf{\Sigma}) \tag{3.45}$$

So, by writing out the various densities involved in Eq. (3.44), we have

$$p(\mathbf{M}|\mathbf{X}_1) = C \exp\{-\tfrac{1}{2}(\mathbf{X}_1 - \mathbf{M})^t \mathbf{\Sigma}^{-1}(\mathbf{X}_1 - \mathbf{M}) \\ - \tfrac{1}{2}(\mathbf{M} - \mathbf{\mu})^t \mathbf{K}^{-1}(\mathbf{M} - \mathbf{\mu})\} \tag{3.46}$$

where C does not depend on **M**. Since the exponent in Eq. (3.46) is a quadric function in **M**, we have verified that $p(\mathbf{M}|\mathbf{X}_1)$ is a normal distribution. By expanding the exponent in Eq. (3.46), it is a straightforward matter to identify the mean vector and covariance matrix

$$\mathbf{\mu}_1 = \mathbf{K}(\mathbf{K} + \mathbf{\Sigma})^{-1}\mathbf{X}_1 + \mathbf{\Sigma}(\mathbf{K} + \mathbf{\Sigma})^{-1}\mathbf{\mu}$$

and $\tag{3.47}$

$$\mathbf{K}_1 = \mathbf{K}(\mathbf{K} + \mathbf{\Sigma})^{-1}\mathbf{\Sigma}$$

If the number of patterns in this training subset were increased to N, we can show by induction that

$$p(\mathbf{M}|\mathbf{X}_1, \mathbf{X}_2, \ldots, \mathbf{X}_N) \sim N(\mathbf{\mu}_N, \mathbf{K}_N) \tag{3.48}$$

where

$$\mathbf{\mu}_N = \frac{\mathbf{\Sigma}}{N}\left(\mathbf{K} + \frac{\mathbf{\Sigma}}{N}\right)^{-1}\mathbf{\mu} + \mathbf{K}\left(\mathbf{K} + \frac{\mathbf{\Sigma}}{N}\right)^{-1}\langle\mathbf{X}\rangle$$
$$\mathbf{K}_N = \mathbf{K}\left(\mathbf{K} + \frac{\mathbf{\Sigma}}{N}\right)^{-1}\frac{\mathbf{\Sigma}}{N} \tag{3.49}$$

PARAMETRIC TRAINING METHODS 61

and the sample mean

$$\langle \mathbf{X} \rangle = \frac{1}{N} \sum_{i=1}^{N} \mathbf{X}_i \qquad (3 \cdot 50)$$

The optimum a posteriori discriminant function (after training on the set $\{\mathbf{X}_1, \mathbf{X}_2, \ldots, \mathbf{X}_N\}$) is then given by Eq. (3·31) with $\mathbf{M}$ replaced by $\mathbf{\mu}_N$ and $\mathbf{\Sigma}$ replaced by $\mathbf{\Sigma} + \mathbf{K}_N$. The process of obtaining $\mathbf{\mu}_N$ from the training set is referred to as *learning the mean vector*.

We note the asymptotic results

$$\lim_{N \to \infty} \mathbf{\mu}_N = \langle \mathbf{X} \rangle$$
$$\lim_{N \to \infty} \mathbf{K}_N = 0 \qquad (3 \cdot 51)$$

Further insight into the process of learning the mean vector can be obtained by considering the special case where $\mathbf{K} = (1/\alpha)\mathbf{\Sigma}$, where α is a positive constant. If α is small, there is much uncertainty (little a priori knowledge) about the mean vector; if α is very large, the mean vector is a priori known to be almost certainly equal to $\mathbf{\mu}$. In this case Eq. (3·49) reduces to

$$\mathbf{\mu}_N = \frac{1}{\alpha + N} [\alpha \mathbf{\mu} + N \langle \mathbf{X} \rangle]$$

and $\qquad (3 \cdot 52)$

$$\mathbf{K}_N = \frac{1}{\alpha + N} \mathbf{\Sigma}$$

If α is small, $\mathbf{\mu}_N$ is closely approximated by the sample mean $\langle \mathbf{X} \rangle$, and $\mathbf{K}_N$ is closely approximated by $\mathbf{\Sigma}/N$. If α is very large, we resist modifying our a priori faith in $\mathbf{\mu}$ as the mean vector, and $\mathbf{K}_N$ is negligible. We can see from these asymptotic relations that, if we are reasonably uncertain about the mean vector ($\alpha < 1$), and if N is reasonably large ($N > 10$), we are quite justified in using the sample mean for $\mathbf{M}$ in Eq. (3·31).

3·12 Bibliographical and historical remarks

A standard statistical text on decision theory is that of Blackwell and Girshick.[1] A short tutorial paper by Abramson[2] is an excellent introduction to the subject.

The example of Sec. 3·5, in which the patterns were composed of independent, random, binary components, follows an unpublished derivation given by J. W. Jones of International Telephone and Telegraph. A similar derivation is given by Minsky.[3] Winder[4] has determined that the weights specified by Eqs. (3·14) and (3·15) of this example will realize only a small percentage of the linearly separable switching functions and suggests another method for determining the weight values from the training set. The restriction to independent components is relaxed by Bahadur,[5] who develops a series expression for the optimum discriminant function.

The multivariate normal distribution is well treated in a book by Anderson.[6] Equation (3·31) for the quadric discriminant functions, optimum for normal patterns, has been previously derived by Anderson[6] and others. A similar derivation motivated by applications to signal detection theory has been given by Kailath.[7] Cooper[8] has extended some of the results of Sec. 3·8 on the optimum classifier for normal patterns to a more general class of density functions, the Pearson functions.

When the number of patterns in a training subset is less than the pattern dimensionality, the sample covariance matrix will be singular as was pointed out in Sec. 3·10. Kanal and Randall[9] discuss this problem and recommend a remedy originally proposed by Harley.[10]

The material in Sec. 3·11 on learning the mean vector of normal patterns is based on the work of Abramson and Braverman.[11] An extension of this work to include learning the covariance matrix of normal patterns has been made by Keehn.[12]

REFERENCES

1 Blackwell, D., and M. A. Girshick: "Theory of Games and Statistical Decisions," John Wiley & Sons, Inc., New York, 1954.

2 Abramson, N.: An Introduction to Bayes Decision Procedures, "Proceedings of Symposium on Decision Theory and Applications to Electronic Equipment Development," vol. 1, *Rome Air Development Center Technical Report* RADC-7R-60-70A, pp. 1–21, April, 1960.

3 Minsky, M.: Steps toward Artificial Intelligence, *Proc. IRE*, vol. 49, no. 1, p. 14, January, 1961.

4 Winder, R. O.: Threshold Logic in Artificial Intelligence, *IEEE Publication S-142, Artificial Intelligence* (a combined preprint of papers presented at the winter general meeting, 1963), pp. 107–128, New York, 1963.

5 Bahadur, R. R.: On Classification Based on Responses to n Dichotomous

Items, in H. Solomon (ed.), "Studies in Item Analysis and Prediction," Stanford University Press, Stanford, California, 1961.
6. Anderson, T. W.: "Introduction to Multivariate Statistical Analysis," John Wiley & Sons, Inc., New York, 1958.
7. Kailath, T.: Correlation Detection of Signals Perturbed by a Random Channel, *Trans. IRE on Info. Theory*, vol. IT-6, no. 3, pp. 361–366, June, 1960.
8. Cooper, P. W.: Hyperplanes, Hyperspheres, and Hyperquadrics as Decision Boundaries, in J. Tou and R. Wilcox (eds.), "Computer and Information Sciences," Spartan Books, Washington, D.C., 1964.
9. Kanal, L. N., and N. C. Randall: Recognition System Design by Statistical Analysis, "Proceedings of the 19th National Conference," *Assoc. for Computing Machinery Publication P*-64, August, 1964.
10. Harley, T. J.: A Small Sample Pseudo-estimate of Covariance Matrices, unpublished Philco Corporation Report, Scientific Laboratory, Blue Bell, Pennsylvania.
11. Abramson, N., and D. Braverman: Learning to Recognize Patterns in a Random Environment, *Trans. IRE on Info. Theory*, vol. IT-8, no. 5, pp. 558–563, September, 1962.
12. Keehn, D. G.: Learning the Mean Vector and Covariance Matrix of Gaussian Signals in Pattern Recognition, *Stanford Electronics Laboratories Technical Report* 2003-6, February, 1963.

CHAPTER 4

SOME NONPARAMETRIC TRAINING METHODS FOR Φ MACHINES

4·1 Nonparametric training of a TLU

In this chapter we shall introduce some specific nonparametric training methods for linear machines (employing linear discriminant functions). We shall be able to apply these methods also to any Φ machine since Φ functions are linear in their parameters. As a basis for our discussion of these training methods we shall first consider the case $R = 2$. Then, the linear machine consists of a threshold logic unit (TLU).

Suppose that we have a finite training set $\mathfrak{X}$ of N patterns and that $\mathfrak{X}$ is divided into two training subsets $\mathfrak{X}_1$ and $\mathfrak{X}_2$. The subset $\mathfrak{X}_1$ contains those patterns belonging to category 1, and $\mathfrak{X}_2$ contains those patterns belonging to category 2. *In this chapter we shall assume that the training subsets are linearly separable.* Based only on this assumption we shall describe procedures for training a TLU to respond with a $+1$ to each of the patterns in $\mathfrak{X}_1$ and with a -1 to each of the patterns in $\mathfrak{X}_2$.

We recall that a TLU implements a hyperplane decision surface which divides the pattern space into two half-spaces. One of these half-spaces is $\mathcal{R}_1$; the other is $\mathcal{R}_2$. The hyperplane separating these half-spaces is determined by the TLU weights $w_1, w_2, \ldots, w_d, w_{d+1}$. Training a TLU to dichotomize correctly the training subsets is equivalent to finding a set of weights such that the hyperplane separates $\mathfrak{X}_1$ and $\mathfrak{X}_2$. The training methods to be described here call for iterative weight adjustments and thus iterative changes in the orientation and position of the hyperplane. A clearer picture of the precise effects of these weight adjustments is provided by an alternative geometric representation of the TLU, which will be discussed next.

4·2 Weight space

Before discussing training methods for a TLU it will be helpful to formulate a geometric representation in which the TLU weight values are the coordinates of a point in a multidimensional space. This space, which we shall call *weight space*, can be considered to be a dual of the pattern space that has been the basis for our discussions up to now. A quite simple and intuitively appealing description of the TLU training methods can be given in terms of the weight-space representation.

Suppose that the TLU has $d + 1$ weights, $w_1, w_2, \ldots, w_d, w_{d+1}$. This set of weights can be represented by a point in a $(d + 1)$-dimensional weight space. The rectangular coordinates of the point are given by the weight values. The $(d + 1)$-dimensional vector $\mathbf{W}$ with components $w_1, w_2, \ldots, w_d, w_{d+1}$, extending from the origin to this point, can also be used to represent the set of weight values. We shall use the symbol $\mathbf{W}$ to denote both the weight vector and the weight point.

We shall retain the concept of a pattern vector, but to simplify the ensuing discussion, we augment the original pattern vector $\mathbf{X}$ by a $(d + 1)$st component whose value is always equal to unity. We shall denote this *augmented* pattern vector by the symbol $\mathbf{Y}$. The components of $\mathbf{Y}$ will be given by $y_1, y_2, \ldots, y_D$, where $D = d + 1$, $y_i = x_i$ for $i = 1, \ldots, D - 1$, and $y_D = +1$.

A linear discriminant function of $\mathbf{X}$ can now be written in terms of $\mathbf{Y}$ in the simple form

$$g(\mathbf{X}) = \mathbf{Y} \cdot \mathbf{W} \tag{4.1}$$

For any pattern* $\mathbf{Y}$, there is a hyperplane in weight space which is the

---

* We sometimes drop the term "augmented," but it is understood whenever we are speaking of $\mathbf{Y}$ as opposed to $\mathbf{X}$.

SOME NONPARAMETRIC TRAINING METHODS FOR Φ MACHINES 67

locus of all weight points for which

$$\mathbf{W} \cdot \mathbf{Y} = 0 \tag{4.2}$$

The hyperplane in weight space defined by Eq. (4·2) for a given pattern vector is called the *pattern hyperplane*. This hyperplane separates the space of weight points into two classes: Those which for the pattern **Y** produce a TLU response of *one* are on one side of the hyperplane, called the *positive* side, and those which produce a TLU response of *minus one* are on the other, or *negative* side. Note that the point representing the weight values $w_1 = 0, w_2 = 0, \ldots, w_D = 0$ satisfies Eq. (4·2) regardless of **Y**. Therefore all pattern hyperplanes pass through the origin of weight space.

Corresponding to the training subsets $\mathfrak{X}_1$ and $\mathfrak{X}_2$ there are subsets of D-dimensional, augmented patterns $\mathcal{Y}_1$ and $\mathcal{Y}_2$. Each element of $\mathcal{Y}_1$ and $\mathcal{Y}_2$ is obtained by augmenting the patterns in $\mathfrak{X}_1$ and $\mathfrak{X}_2$, respectively. We shall denote the union of $\mathcal{Y}_1$ and $\mathcal{Y}_2$ by the symbol $\mathcal{Y}$. Our assumption that $\mathfrak{X}_1$ and $\mathfrak{X}_2$ are linearly separable means that a weight vector **W** exists, called the *solution* weight vector, such that

$$\mathbf{Y} \cdot \mathbf{W} > 0 \quad \text{for each } \mathbf{Y} \text{ in } \mathcal{Y}_1$$
and $\tag{4.3}$
$$\mathbf{Y} \cdot \mathbf{W} < 0 \quad \text{for each } \mathbf{Y} \text{ in } \mathcal{Y}_2$$

Corresponding to the N augmented patterns in the training set $\mathcal{Y}$ there is a set of N pattern hyperplanes which divide weight space into a number of different regions. The response of the TLU to any pattern depends on where (which side of the pattern hyperplane) the TLU weight point **W** resides. As **W** is varied, the TLU responses to some of the patterns will change if **W** crosses any of the pattern hyperplanes and thus leaves a region. Therefore, each region in weight space corresponds to a different linear dichotomy of the N patterns, and, conversely, a dichotomy of the patterns in $\mathcal{Y}$ is a linear dichotomy only if there is a region in weight space corresponding to it.* For any given linear dichotomy, the corre-

---

* If we count the number of regions in weight space formed by N augmented pattern hyperplanes, we obtain the number of dichotomies of N d-dimensional patterns implementable by a TLU, that is, the number of linear dichotomies of N patterns. Thus we have an alternative method for computing $L(N,d)$.

It is a straightforward matter to calculate the maximum number of regions formed by N hyperplanes all passing through the origin of a D-dimensional space. Suppose we have N hyperplanes intersecting at a point (the origin) in a D-dimensional space. Let the number of regions into which the N planes divide this space be denoted by $R(N,D)$. Suppose we have $N - 1$ hyperplanes creating $R(N - 1, D)$ regions. How many more are created by adding another hyperplane? The Nth hyperplane

SOME NONPARAMETRIC TRAINING METHODS FOR Φ MACHINES

sponding region in weight space is called the *solution region*. It is a convex region containing all of the solution weight points **W** satisfying inequality (4·3).

These ideas are illustrated in Fig. 4·1 for a two-dimensional weight space ($D = 2$). In this example, the small arrows attached to the pattern hyperplanes (lines) indicate the positive side of each hyperplane. The

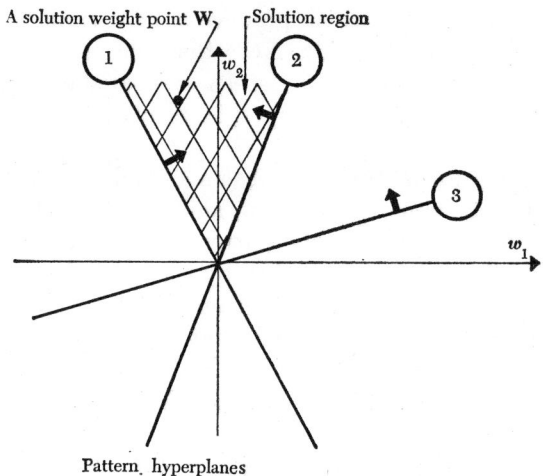

FIGURE 4 · 1 A two-dimensional weight space with three pattern hyperplanes

encircled numbers attached to the hyperplanes indicate the number of the pattern. Thus, the solution region and the solution weight point **W** indicated in the figure apply to the linear dichotomy for which augmented patterns number one, two, and three all belong to the set $\mathcal{Y}_1$. Each of these patterns would cause a TLU response of $+1$ if the TLU had weights given by the components of this solution weight point.

---

intersects the other $N - 1$ hyperplanes in at most $N - 1$ hyperplanes of $D - 2$ dimensions. These $N - 1$ lower-dimensional hyperplanes divide the Nth hyperplane into at most $R(N - 1, D - 1)$ regions since this is the same problem except one dimension lower. Now, each one of these $R(N - 1, D - 1)$ regions on the Nth hyperplane divides one of the original $R(N - 1, D)$ regions in the D-dimensional space into two parts. Therefore, the addition of the Nth plane can add at most $R(N - 1, D - 1)$ new regions. This fact gives us the relation

$$R(N,D) = R(N - 1, D) + R(N - 1, D - 1)$$

which is the same as that developed in Chapter 2.

4·3 TLU training procedures

Suppose that we have a linear dichotomy of $\mathcal{Y}$ with two subsets $\mathcal{Y}_1$ and $\mathcal{Y}_2$ and that for some pattern $\mathbf{Y}$ in $\mathcal{Y}$, a TLU with a weight vector $\mathbf{W}$ has a response which is either erroneous ($\mathbf{Y} \cdot \mathbf{W} < 0$) or undefined ($\mathbf{Y} \cdot \mathbf{W} = 0$). That is, $\mathbf{W}$ is either on the negative side of or on the pattern hyperplane corresponding to $\mathbf{Y}$. This error can be rectified by moving $\mathbf{W}$ to the positive side of the pattern hyperplane. The most direct path to the other side is along a line normal to the pattern hyperplane. Such a motion can be achieved by adding the augmented pattern vector $\mathbf{Y}$ to $\mathbf{W}$ to create a new weight vector $\mathbf{W}'$. Each TLU weight component is adjusted by an amount proportional to the corresponding component of the augmented pattern. That is,

$$\mathbf{W}' = \mathbf{W} + c\mathbf{Y} \tag{4·4}$$

where c is a positive number called the *correction increment*. It controls the extent of the adjustment. For sufficiently large c, the weight point will cross the pattern hyperplane, and $\mathbf{Y} \cdot \mathbf{W}'$ will be correctly positive. If $\mathbf{W}$ were incorrectly on the positive side of a pattern hyperplane, it could be moved to the negative side by subtracting from the weight vector (instead of adding to it) the correction increment times the augmented pattern vector.

In the nonparametric training methods to be discussed in this book, we shall be concerned with iterative procedures employing such a motion of a *trial* weight point along a normal to a pattern hyperplane. Methods based on this procedure for weight-vector adjustment do exist for training a TLU to perform perfect separations of the training subsets when such separations are possible. In this section we shall discuss in detail some of these methods. They are called *error-correction* training procedures.

In the error-correction training procedures, the training patterns are presented to the trainable TLU one at a time for trial. The trial consists of comparing the actual response of the TLU with the desired response dictated by the category of the pattern. The patterns may be tried in any order, but it may be necessary that each pattern in the training set be tried several times. The patterns may be presented by cycling through the training set, over and over, or the patterns may be presented in some random order as long as the trial of each one recurs. When the patterns are presented cyclically, each pass through the training set is called an *iteration*.

Before training begins, the TLU weights may be preset to any convenient values or they may be set to values selected at random. If the TLU responds correctly to a pattern (i.e., with the desired response), no adjustments are made to the TLU weights, and another pattern is presented for trial. Suppose that the TLU with present weight vector **W** responds incorrectly to an augmented pattern vector **Y**. The weight vector is then changed to a new weight vector **W**′, as follows:

$$\begin{aligned} \mathbf{W}' &= \mathbf{W} + c\mathbf{Y} && \text{if } \mathbf{Y} \text{ belonged to category 1} \\ \mathbf{W}' &= \mathbf{W} - c\mathbf{Y} && \text{if } \mathbf{Y} \text{ belonged to category 2} \end{aligned} \qquad (4\cdot5)$$

where c is the correction increment, which will be discussed more fully below.

There are several types of error-correction procedures. We shall mention three of them here. These differ solely in the interpretation to be given to the value of the correction increment. For one of them, called the *fixed-increment rule*, c is taken to be any fixed number greater than zero. When c is equal to one, for example, each weight is altered by the addition (or subtraction) of the corresponding pattern component. This adjustment may or may not actually correct the error for the pattern, depending on the value of $\mathbf{W} \cdot \mathbf{Y}$ in relation to c.

Variations of the above procedure make c dependent on the quantity $\mathbf{W} \cdot \mathbf{Y}$, the amount by which the weighted input combination differs from the threshold of zero. In one case, c is taken to be the smallest integer which will make the value of $\mathbf{W} \cdot \mathbf{Y}$ cross the threshold of zero. That is, we desire that

$$\mathbf{W}' \cdot \mathbf{Y} = (\mathbf{W} + c\mathbf{Y}) \cdot \mathbf{Y} > 0$$

for $\mathbf{W} \cdot \mathbf{Y}$ erroneously nonpositive and (4·6)

$$\mathbf{W}' \cdot \mathbf{Y} = (\mathbf{W} - c\mathbf{Y}) \cdot \mathbf{Y} < 0$$

for $\mathbf{W} \cdot \mathbf{Y}$ erroneously nonnegative.

Therefore, c must be the smallest integer greater than $|\mathbf{W} \cdot \mathbf{Y}|/\mathbf{Y} \cdot \mathbf{Y}$. After the weights have been adjusted by this rule, the *absolute correction rule*, the TLU response will agree with the desired response. It is readily seen that the absolute correction rule leads to the same results as does the fixed-increment rule with $c = 1$ if, in the latter, the presentation of each pattern is repeated until the pattern is categorized correctly.

In another variation, it is desired to set c at a value such that the quantity $|\mathbf{W} \cdot \mathbf{Y} - \mathbf{W}' \cdot \mathbf{Y}|$ is a certain positive fraction λ of $|\mathbf{W} \cdot \mathbf{Y}|$. From the results of Sec. 2·6, we observe that $|\mathbf{W} \cdot \mathbf{Y}|$ is proportional to the normal distance between the weight point **W** and the pattern hyperplane corresponding to **Y**. The quantity $|\mathbf{W} \cdot \mathbf{Y} - \mathbf{W}' \cdot \mathbf{Y}|$ is then proportional to the distance between the old weight point **W** and the new weight point **W**′. Therefore, λ is the fraction of the distance to the pattern hyperplane traversed in moving from **W** to **W**′. In this rule, the *fractional correction* rule, c is equal to $\lambda |\mathbf{W} \cdot \mathbf{Y}|/\mathbf{Y} \cdot \mathbf{Y}$. If $\lambda > 1$, then the TLU response after adjustment will be the desired response.

In each of the procedures just described, the value of c determines how *far* the weight point is moved. We have distinguished three cases. In one case, c is a fixed constant so that the distance moved toward a particular pattern hyperplane is always the same. This fixed distance may or may not be sufficient to cross the pattern hyperplane and thus correct the error. In another case, c is chosen to be just large enough to

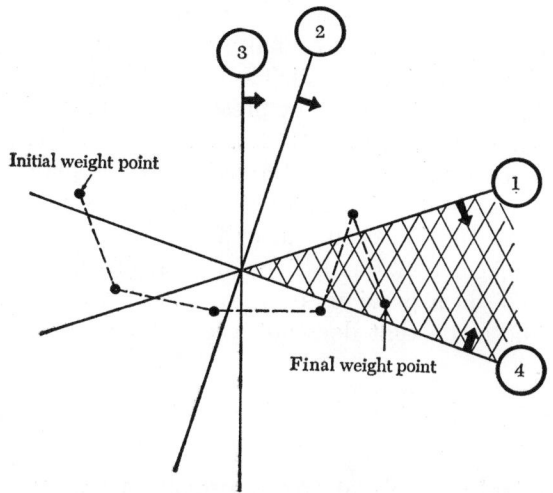

FIGURE 4·2 A graphical illustration of error-correction training

guarantee that the pattern hyperplane is crossed and the response corrected. In the third case c is so chosen that the distance moved is some fixed fraction of the original distance of the weight vector from the hyperplane. For $\lambda = 0$, the weight point is not moved at all; for $\lambda = 1$, the weight point is moved to the pattern hyperplane; and for $\lambda = 2$, the weight point is reflected across the pattern hyperplane to a point an equal distance on the other side.

The complete error-correction training procedure can, therefore, be described as a sequential examination of a set of pattern hyperplanes. For each pattern hyperplane, one inquires whether or not the weight point is on the desired side. If it is on the desired side, the next pattern hyperplane in the training set is examined. If it is not, the weight point is moved perpendicularly toward this plane (e.g., across it), and then the next pattern in the set is examined. The process continues until a solution weight vector is reached. It is one of the central mathematical results of the theory of trainable pattern-classifying machines that each of the three

72 SOME NONPARAMETRIC TRAINING METHODS FOR Φ MACHINES

variations of the error-correction rule is convergent. By convergent we mean that when the pattern training subsets are linearly separable, the sequence of TLU weight vectors produced by the training procedure converges toward a solution weight vector. The fixed-increment and absolute correction rules are guaranteed to produce a solution weight vector after only a *finite* number of weight-vector adjustments. The convergence proofs, to be given in Chapter 5, require only that $c > 0$ or $0 < \lambda \leq 2$, depending on the variant used.

An extremely simple graphical example of error-correction training is illustrated in Fig. 4·2. There are four patterns represented by pattern hyperplanes in weight space. The small arrows attached to these planes in this case indicate the side on which a TLU weight vector will give the *desired* response. The patterns will be presented cyclically in the following order: 1, 2, 3, 4, 1, 2, 3, 4, 1, 2, 3, 4, ... The pattern numbers are indicated in the circles attached to the pattern hyperplanes. It is desired to converge to a weight point in the shaded (solution) region. In this simple example, a solution occurs after five adjustments. Note that an adjustment to correct the response for one pattern may very well undo a correction made on a previous pattern. Eventually, however, one last correction will be made that does not affect the correct response to the other patterns.

4 · 4 A numerical example of error-correction training

It is also instructive to trace through a numerical example of the error-correction training rule; we shall do so for a set of three-dimensional patterns with binary components using the fixed-increment correction rule with $c = 1$. The training set of augmented pattern vectors and their desired responses is shown below.

y_1	y_2	y_3	y_4	Desired response
0	1	1	1	−1
0	0	0	1	1
1	0	0	1	1
1	0	1	1	1
0	0	1	1	−1
1	1	0	1	1
1	1	1	1	−1
0	1	0	1	−1

SOME NONPARAMETRIC TRAINING METHODS FOR Φ MACHINES

The fact that the dichotomy is linear can be readily determined by observing in Fig. 4·3 that a separating hyperplane does exist. Therefore, we should expect the training rule to terminate successfully. Let the initial values of the four weights all be equal to zero, and then cycle through the pattern list until a solution is reached. The training history for this example is detailed in Table 4·1. We note that termination occurs during the

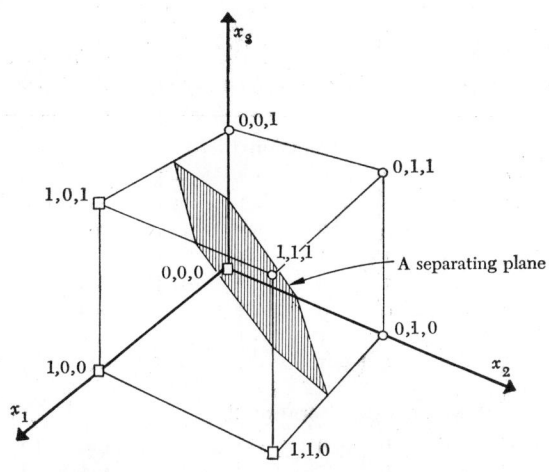

○ Patterns requiring −1 response

□ Patterns requiring +1 response

FIGURE 4·3 A plane which correctly partitions eight three-dimensional patterns

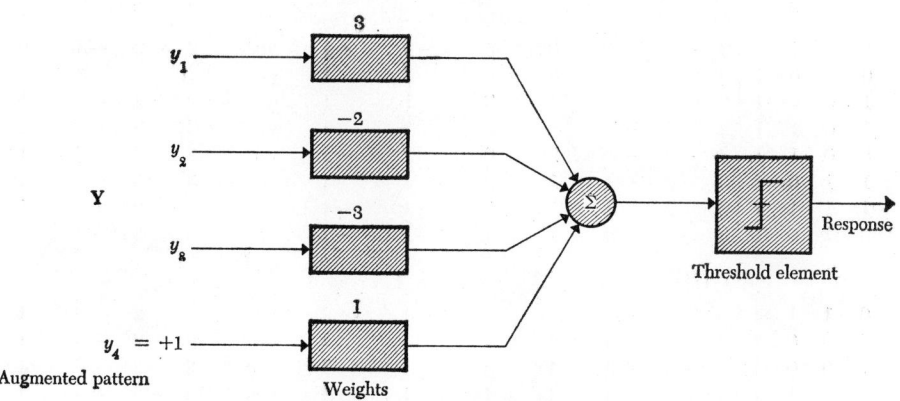

FIGURE 4·4 A TLU trained to respond correctly to eight three-dimensional patterns

fourth iteration after a total of 29 pattern presentations and 13 weight-vector adjustments. The trained TLU which responds as desired to all eight patterns is represented schematically in Fig. 4·4.

TABLE 4 · 1 Record of fixed-increment error-correction training for a three-dimensional example

Augmented pattern $y_1\ y_2\ y_3\ y_4$	Weight vector $w_1\ \ w_2\ \ w_3\ \ w_4$	$\mathbf{W}\cdot\mathbf{Y}$	TLU response	Desired response	Adjustment?	New weight vector $w_1\ \ w_2\ \ w_3\ \ w_4$
		Iteration 1				
0 1 1 1	0 0 0 0	0	*	−1	yes	0 −1 −1 −1
0 0 0 1	0 −1 −1 −1	−1	−1	1	yes	0 −1 −1 0
1 0 0 1	0 −1 −1 0	0	*	1	yes	1 −1 −1 1
1 0 1 1	1 −1 −1 1	1	1	1	no	1 −1 −1 1
0 0 1 1	1 −1 −1 1	0	*	−1	yes	1 −1 −2 0
1 1 0 1	1 −1 −2 0	0	*	1	yes	2 0 −2 1
1 1 1 1	2 0 −2 1	1	1	−1	yes	1 −1 −3 0
0 1 0 1	1 −1 −3 0	−1	−1	−1	no	1 −1 −3 0
		Iteration 2				
0 1 1 1	1 −1 −3 0	−4	−1	−1	no	1 −1 −3 0
0 0 0 1	1 −1 −3 0	0	*	1	yes	1 −1 −3 1
1 0 0 1	1 −1 −3 1	2	1	1	no	1 −1 −3 1
1 0 1 1	1 −1 −3 1	−1	−1	1	yes	2 −1 −2 2
0 0 1 1	2 −1 −2 2	0	*	−1	yes	2 −1 −3 1
1 1 0 1	2 −1 −3 1	2	1	1	no	2 −1 −3 1
1 1 1 1	2 −1 −3 1	−1	−1	−1	no	2 −1 −3 1
0 1 0 1	2 −1 −3 1	0	*	−1	yes	2 −2 −3 0
		Iteration 3				
0 1 1 1	2 −2 −3 0	−5	−1	−1	no	2 −2 −3 0
0 0 0 1	2 −2 −3 0	0	*	1	yes	2 −2 −3 1
1 0 0 1	2 −2 −3 1	3	1	1	no	2 −2 −3 1
1 0 1 1	2 −2 −3 1	0	*	1	yes	3 −2 −2 2
0 0 1 1	3 −2 −2 2	0	*	−1	yes	3 −2 −3 1
1 1 0 1	3 −2 −3 1	2	1	1	no	3 −2 −3 1
1 1 1 1	3 −2 −3 1	−1	−1	−1	no	3 −2 −3 1
0 1 0 1	3 −2 −3 1	−1	−1	−1	no	3 −2 −3 1
		Iteration 4				
0 1 1 1	3 −2 −3 1	−4	−1	−1	no	3 −2 −3 1
0 0 0 1	3 −2 −3 1	1	1	1	no	3 −2 −3 1
1 0 0 1	3 −2 −3 1	4	1	1	no	3 −2 −3 1
1 0 1 1	3 −2 −3 1	1	1	1	no	3 −2 −3 1
0 0 1 1	3 −2 −3 1	−2	−1	−1	no	3 −2 −3 1

* Indicates undefined response.

4·5 An error-correction training procedure for $R > 2$

A linear machine for classifying patterns belonging to more than two categories was defined in Chapter 2. It consists of R linear discriminators and a maximum selector (Fig. 2·1). Each discriminant function can be represented as the dot product of a weight vector with an augmented pattern vector; that is,

$$g_i(\mathbf{X}) = \mathbf{W}^{(i)} \cdot \mathbf{Y} \quad \text{for } i = 1, \ldots, R \tag{4·7}$$

Simple extensions of the training procedures already discussed can be used to train a general linear machine.

Suppose we have a set $\mathcal{Y}$ of augmented training patterns divided into subsets $\mathcal{Y}_1, \mathcal{Y}_2, \ldots, \mathcal{Y}_R$ which are linearly separable. The subset $\mathcal{Y}_i$ contains all training patterns in $\mathcal{Y}$ belonging to category i. We desire to train the linear machine by adjusting its weight vectors so that it responds correctly to every pattern in $\mathcal{Y}$. A response to a pattern in category i is correct only if the ith discriminant is the largest.

A *generalized* error-correction procedure can be used to train the general linear machine and thus find (solution) weight vectors when they exist. In this procedure, each pattern in $\mathcal{Y}$ is presented one at a time in any sequence. Arbitrary initial weight vectors are selected for the machine, and adjustments of these are made whenever the machine responds incorrectly to any pattern. Suppose that a pattern $\mathbf{Y}$ belonging to category i is presented with the result that some discriminant, say the jth ($j \neq i$), is larger than the ith. That is, the machine erroneously places $\mathbf{Y}$ in category j. The weight vectors used by both the ith and jth discriminators are then modified by the addition and subtraction, respectively, of the pattern vector, $\mathbf{Y}$. Let the ith and jth weight vectors prior to modification be denoted by $\mathbf{W}^{(i)}$ and $\mathbf{W}^{(j)}$, respectively. The adjusted weight vectors $\mathbf{W}^{(i)\prime}$ and $\mathbf{W}^{(j)\prime}$ are then

$$\mathbf{W}^{(i)\prime} = \mathbf{W}^{(i)} + c\mathbf{Y}$$
and
$$\mathbf{W}^{(j)\prime} = \mathbf{W}^{(j)} - c\mathbf{Y} \tag{4·8}$$

where c is again the correction increment. The effect of the adjustment is to increase the value of the ith discriminant while decreasing the value of the jth discriminant. We shall prove in the next chapter that the generalized error-correction procedure is guaranteed to find a set of solution weight vectors after only a finite number of adjustments if such a set exists. Observe that for $R = 2$ the generalized error-correction procedure is identical with the one discussed previously.

4 · 6 Applications to Φ machines

The training methods that have been discussed in this chapter have all been phrased to apply to linear machines. We can easily observe that these same methods can be used to train Φ machines. From Chapter 2 we recall that a Φ machine can be implemented by a Φ processor followed by a linear machine. The Φ processor converts the set $\mathfrak{X}$ of d-dimensional pattern vectors into a set $\mathfrak{F}$ of M-dimensional vectors by the mapping $\mathbf{F} = \mathbf{F}(\mathbf{X})$.

The error-correction training methods for linear machines can be used to find an $(M + 1)$-dimensional solution weight point for any linear dichotomy of the set $\mathfrak{F}$ and thus a Φ dichotomy of the set $\mathfrak{X}$. Therefore, a machine employing discriminant functions belonging to any given Φ function family can be trained to implement any dichotomy of $\mathfrak{X}$ that can possibly be implemented using a discriminant function belonging to the same family. The training of a Φ machine is accomplished by training only the linear part; the Φ processor remains fixed.

Recognizing that Φ functions comprise a large set of useful discriminant function families, the error-correction training methods indeed represent quite general and powerful techniques.

4 · 7 Bibliographical and historical remarks

The idea of a threshold logic unit with adjustable weights resulted from combining two concepts proposed during the 1940s. The first concept was that an on-off threshold device was a simplified model of a neuron or nerve cell. The main proponents of this idea were McCulloch and Pitts.[1] The second concept was that long-term memory in animals depended on changes in the synaptic junctions between neurons. The main proponent of this idea was Hebb.[2]

Rochester et al.[3] and Farley and Clark[4] and others soon afterward proposed networks of threshold devices connected through adjustable weights (synapses) as model nerve nets capable of learning. The main credit for the successful synthesis of these two concepts into the idea of a trainable TLU must go to Rosenblatt,[5] who proposed and used the trainable TLU as the learning element of a system he called an α perceptron. Properties of the α perceptron and other TLU networks are well documented in a book[6] by Rosenblatt. An article by Block[7] provides an excellent introduction to perceptrons.

During this period Widrow[8] was pursuing engineering applications of trainable TLUs which he called ADALINES (for *ada*ptive *line*ar devices). An account of some of these applications is contained in a paper by Widrow et al.[9]

The weight-space representation introduced in Sec. 4·2 to describe the properties of a TLU has been employed by Ridgway[10] and also by Motzkin and Schoenberg.[11] The alternative derivation of $L(N,d)$ given in the footnote on page 67 follows the derivation by Cameron.[12]

The error-correction training procedures discussed in Sec. 4·3 stem from a variety of sources. The fixed-increment and absolute correction rules were first proposed by Rosenblatt,[13] although Widrow and Hoff[8] introduced a similar rule at substantially the same time. Ridgway[10] later suggested a modification of the Widrow-Hoff rule which rendered it substantially the same as the absolute correction rule. Motzkin and Schoenberg[11] proposed what we have called the fractional correction rule as a method for the solution of linear inequalities. In analogy with the relaxation methods for solving linear equalities, they speak of *underrelaxation* and *overrelaxation* for the cases of $\lambda < 1$ and $\lambda > 1$, respectively. The generalized error-correction training procedure for $R > 2$ was suggested by C. Kesler at Cornell University.

Proof that these training procedures will either terminate or converge are given in Chapter 5. The historical background of these proofs will be discussed in Sec. 5·7.

REFERENCES

1. McCulloch, W., and W. Pitts: A Logical Calculus of the Ideas Immanent in Nervous Activity, *Bulletin of Math. Biophysics*, vol. 5, pp. 115–133, 1943.
2. Hebb, D.: "Organization of Behavior," Science Editions, Inc., New York, 1961.
3. Rochester, N., et al.: Tests on a Cell Assembly Theory of the Action of the Brain Using a Large Digital Computer, *Trans. IRE on Info. Theory*, vol. IT-2, no. 3, pp. 80–93, September, 1956.
4. Farley, B., and W. Clark: Simulation of Self-organizing Systems by Digital Computer, *Trans. IRE on Info. Theory*, PGIT-4, pp. 76–84, September, 1954.
5. Rosenblatt, F.: The Perceptron: A Perceiving and Recognizing Automaton, Project PARA, *Cornell Aeronautical Laboratory Report* 85-460-1, January, 1957.

6 ———: "Principles of Neurodynamics: Perceptrons and the Theory of Brain Mechanisms," Spartan Books, Washington, D.C., 1961.
7 Block, H.: The Perceptron: A Model for Brain Functioning, I., *Reviews of Modern Physics*, vol. 34, pp. 123–135, January, 1962.
8 Widrow, B., and M. E. Hoff: Adaptive Switching Circuits, *Stanford Electronics Laboratories Technical Report* 1553-1, Stanford University, Stanford, California, June 30, 1960.
9 Widrow, B., et al.: Practical Applications for Adaptive Data-processing Systems, 1963 *WESCON Paper* 11.4, August, 1963.
10 Ridgway, W. C.: An Adaptive Logic System with Generalizing Properties, *Stanford Electronics Laboratories Technical Report* 1556-1, prepared under Air Force Contract AF 33(616)-7726, Stanford University, Stanford, California, April, 1962.
11 Motzkin, T. S., and I. J. Schoenberg: The Relaxation Method for Linear Inequalities, *Canadian Journal of Mathematics*, vol. 6, no. 3, pp. 393–404, 1954.
12 Cameron, S. H.: An Estimate of the Complexity Requisite in a Universal Decision Network, "Proceedings of 1960 Bionics Symposium," *Wright Air Development Division Technical Report* 60-600, pp. 197–211, December, 1960.
13 Rosenblatt, F.: On the Convergence of Reinforcement Procedures in Simple Perceptrons, *Cornell Aeronautical Laboratory Report VG*-1196-*G*-4, Buffalo, New York, February, 1960.

CHAPTER 5

TRAINING THEOREMS

5·1 The fundamental training theorem

In this chapter we shall formally state and prove some theorems about the training procedures mentioned in Chapter 4. These theorems form the core of the theory of iterative nonparametric training methods, and their consequences are applicable to the whole class of Φ discriminant functions. The first theorem is really a theorem about training procedures for two-category pattern classifiers, but Theorem 5·2 extends its applicability to R-category machines.

Let $\mathcal{Y}_1$ be the subset $\{\mathbf{Y}_1^{(1)}, \mathbf{Y}_2^{(1)}, \ldots, \mathbf{Y}_{N_1}^{(1)}\}$ of training patterns belonging to category 1. Let $\mathcal{Y}_2$ be the subset $\{\mathbf{Y}_1^{(2)}, \mathbf{Y}_2^{(2)}, \ldots, \mathbf{Y}_{N_2}^{(2)}\}$ of training patterns belonging to category 2. The union of these two subsets is the complete training set $\mathcal{Y}$. We assume that the sets $\mathcal{Y}_1$ and $\mathcal{Y}_2$ are linearly separable. That is, a solution vector $\mathbf{W}$ exists such that

$$\mathbf{Y} \cdot \mathbf{W} > 0 \quad \text{for each } \mathbf{Y} \epsilon \mathcal{Y}_1$$

and   (5·1)

$$\mathbf{Y} \cdot \mathbf{W} < 0 \quad \text{for each } \mathbf{Y} \epsilon \mathcal{Y}_2$$

TRAINING THEOREMS

A *training sequence* on $\mathcal{Y}$, denoted by S_Y, is any infinite sequence of patterns

$$S_Y = \mathbf{Y}_1, \mathbf{Y}_2, \ldots, \mathbf{Y}_k, \ldots \tag{5.2}$$

such that

1. Each $\mathbf{Y}_k$ in S_Y is a member of $\mathcal{Y}$.
2. Every element of $\mathcal{Y}$ occurs infinitely often in S_Y.

The training problem for a two-category linear machine given training subsets $\mathcal{Y}_1$ and $\mathcal{Y}_2$ is to find a $\mathbf{W}$ such that inequalities (5.1) are satisfied. We shall solve this problem by generating a sequence of weight vectors $S_W = \mathbf{W}_1, \mathbf{W}_2, \mathbf{W}_3, \ldots, \mathbf{W}_k, \ldots$ such that, for some index k_0, $\mathbf{W}_{k_0} = \mathbf{W}_{k_0+1} = \mathbf{W}_{k_0+2} = \cdots$ satisfies inequalities (5.1). The *initial weight vector* $\mathbf{W}_1$ is arbitrary. We shall be interested here in sequences S_W, which are recursively generated from a training sequence S_Y by the following rules:

1. If the kth member of the training sequence $\mathbf{Y}_k$ is correctly classified using the kth member of the weight-vector sequence $\mathbf{W}_k$, then the $(k + 1)$st member of the weight-vector sequence is the same as the kth member. That is,

$$\begin{aligned}\mathbf{W}_{k+1} &= \mathbf{W}_k \quad \text{if } \mathbf{Y}_k \cdot \mathbf{W}_k > 0 \text{ and } \mathbf{Y}_k \in \mathcal{Y}_1 \\ \mathbf{W}_{k+1} &= \mathbf{W}_k \quad \text{if } \mathbf{Y}_k \cdot \mathbf{W}_k < 0 \text{ and } \mathbf{Y}_k \in \mathcal{Y}_2\end{aligned} \tag{5.3}$$

2. Otherwise, the $(k + 1)$st member of the weight-vector sequence is given by

$$\begin{aligned}\mathbf{W}_{k+1} &= \mathbf{W}_k - c_k \mathbf{Y}_k \quad \text{if } \mathbf{Y}_k \cdot \mathbf{W}_k \geq 0 \text{ and } \mathbf{Y}_k \in \mathcal{Y}_2 \\ \mathbf{W}_{k+1} &= \mathbf{W}_k + c_k \mathbf{Y}_k \quad \text{if } \mathbf{Y}_k \cdot \mathbf{W}_k \leq 0 \text{ and } \mathbf{Y}_k \in \mathcal{Y}_1\end{aligned} \tag{5.4}$$

or

where the correction increment c_k is a positive number, possibly depending on k. That is, the $(k + 1)$st weight vector depends only on the kth pattern, the correction increment, and the previous weight vector. The weight vector $\mathbf{W}_k$ is changed only if $\mathbf{Y}_k \cdot \mathbf{W}_k$ is equal to zero or has the incorrect sign relative to the category of $\mathbf{Y}_k$. The sequence of weight vectors S_W is therefore completely determined by the correction increments c_k, the initial weight vector $\mathbf{W}_1$, and the training sequence S_Y.

The rule for changing the weight vector [Eqs. (5.3) and (5.4)] is an error-correction procedure. If $c_k = c > 0$ is a constant not dependent on k, then the rule is a fixed-increment error-correction procedure. Using the foregoing definitions we now have the following theorem.

Theorem 5·1

Let the training subsets $\mathcal{Y}_1$ and $\mathcal{Y}_2$ be linearly separable. Let S_W be the weight-vector sequence generated by any training sequence S_Y, using the fixed-increment error-correction procedure and beginning with any initial weight vector $\mathbf{W}_1$. Then, for some finite index k_0,

$$\mathbf{W}_{k_0} = \mathbf{W}_{k_0+1} = \mathbf{W}_{k_0+2} = \cdots$$

is a solution vector.

Discussion

The value of the fixed correction increment c is clearly unimportant so long as it is positive. If the theorem were true for $c = 1$, it would also be true for $c \neq 1$, since c can be used to scale the pattern vectors without changing their separability. For simplicity in the proofs to follow we shall therefore take $c = 1$.

A slightly modified theorem can also be proved quite simply as a result of Theorem 5·1. In the modified theorem we use an *absolute error-correction procedure* instead of the fixed-increment error-correction procedure. In the absolute error-correction procedure, the value of c_k is taken to be the smallest integer for which $c_k \mathbf{Y}_k \cdot \mathbf{Y}_k > |\mathbf{W}_k \cdot \mathbf{Y}_k|$. With this procedure, if $\mathbf{Y}_k \cdot \mathbf{W}_k$ has an incorrect sign, $\mathbf{Y}_k \cdot \mathbf{W}_{k+1}$ would have the correct sign. The modified theorem is proved quite simply by showing that the absolute error-correction procedure is the same as the fixed-increment procedure for a special training sequence. The special training sequence is generated as follows: If $\mathbf{Y}_k \cdot \mathbf{W}_k$ has an incorrect sign, then $\mathbf{Y}_{k+1} = \mathbf{Y}_k$. That is, each pattern is presented to the TLU until that pattern is classified correctly.

Theorem 5·1 enjoys the reputation of having been proved and re-proved in many seemingly different ways. Two of these proofs, each with a great deal of intuitive appeal, will be given here after we introduce some simplifying notation and reinterpret the theorem accordingly.

5·2 Notation

Let the set $\mathcal{Y}_2'$ be the set consisting of the negatives of the patterns in $\mathcal{Y}_2$. That is

$$\mathcal{Y}_2' = \{-\mathbf{Y}_1^{(2)}, -\mathbf{Y}_2^{(2)}, \ldots, -\mathbf{Y}_{N_2}^{(2)}\} \tag{5·5}$$

The *adjusted* training set $\mathcal{Y}'$ is the union of $\mathcal{Y}_1$ and $\mathcal{Y}_2'$.

82 TRAINING THEOREMS

A set of vectors $\mathcal{Y}'$ will be called *linearly contained* if and only if there exists a vector $\mathbf{W}$, called a *solution weight vector*, such that

$$\mathbf{Y} \cdot \mathbf{W} > 0 \qquad \text{for each } \mathbf{Y} \text{ in } \mathcal{Y}' \tag{5.6}$$

Clearly, $\mathcal{Y}'$ is linearly contained if and only if $\mathcal{Y}_1$ and $\mathcal{Y}_2$ are linearly separable. Furthermore, any $\mathbf{W}$ which satisfies inequality (5·6) will also satisfy the inequalities (5·1).

Let $S_{Y'} = \mathbf{Y}_1', \mathbf{Y}_2', \ldots, \mathbf{Y}_k', \ldots$ be a training sequence on the adjusted pattern set $\mathcal{Y}'$. Each element of the sequence $S_{Y'}$ is obtained from the corresponding sequence S_Y by the relations

$$\begin{aligned}\mathbf{Y}_k' &= \mathbf{Y}_k &\text{if } \mathbf{Y}_k \in \mathcal{Y}_1 \\ \mathbf{Y}_k' &= -\mathbf{Y}_k &\text{if } \mathbf{Y}_k \in \mathcal{Y}_2\end{aligned} \tag{5.7}$$

The fixed-increment error-correction weight-vector sequence S_W can now be produced recursively from the training sequence $S_{\mathcal{Y}'}$ by the simplified rule

$$\begin{aligned}\mathbf{W}_{k+1} &= \mathbf{W}_k &\text{if } \mathbf{Y}_k' \cdot \mathbf{W}_k > 0 \\ \mathbf{W}_{k+1} &= \mathbf{W}_k + \mathbf{Y}_k' &\text{if } \mathbf{Y}_k' \cdot \mathbf{W}_k \leq 0\end{aligned} \tag{5.8}$$

where c_k is assumed equal to unity. Each time the weight vector is actually changed is called a *step*.

The proof of Theorem 5·1 is further simplified if we omit from the training sequence $S_{Y'}$ any patterns $\mathbf{Y}_k'$ for which $\mathbf{W}_{k+1} = \mathbf{W}_k$, i.e., for which $\mathbf{Y}_k' \cdot \mathbf{W}_k > 0$. Let us relabel the remaining patterns in the sequence by the symbols $\hat{\mathbf{Y}}_1, \hat{\mathbf{Y}}_2, \ldots, \hat{\mathbf{Y}}_k, \ldots$. We shall denote this *reduced* training sequence by the symbol $S_{\hat{Y}}$.

If we now begin with the same initial weight vector $\mathbf{W}_1$ as before and apply the fixed-increment error-correction rule with the reduced training sequence, we will generate a *reduced* weight-vector sequence $S_{\hat{W}} = \hat{\mathbf{W}}_1, \hat{\mathbf{W}}_2, \ldots, \hat{\mathbf{W}}_k, \ldots$. In $S_{\hat{W}}$, $\hat{\mathbf{W}}_1 = \mathbf{W}_1$, and $\hat{\mathbf{W}}_k$ is the result of $k - 1$ steps; $S_{\hat{W}}$ will have no repetitions and will therefore *terminate* at the k_0th step if $\hat{\mathbf{W}}_{k_0+1}$ is a weight vector which satisfies inequality (5·6).

Theorem 5·1 will be proved if we prove that $S_{\hat{W}}$ terminates.

5·3 Proof 1

The following proof results from conflicting bounds on the growth rate of the length of the weight vector during the fixed-increment error-correction process.

Let $S_{\hat{Y}}$ be a reduced training sequence on the linearly contained training set $\mathcal{Y}'$. Let $S_{\hat{W}}$ be the reduced weight-vector sequence resulting from the application of the fixed-increment error-correction rule beginning with initial weight vector $\hat{W}_1$.

Since for each $\hat{Y}_j$ in $S_{\hat{Y}}$ and $\hat{W}_j$ in $S_{\hat{W}}$, $\hat{Y}_j \cdot \hat{W}_j \leq 0$, we have from Eq. (5·8)

$$\hat{W}_{k+1} = \hat{W}_1 + \hat{Y}_1 + \hat{Y}_2 + \cdots + \hat{Y}_k \qquad (5\cdot 9)$$

We shall prove the theorem for the case $\hat{W}_1 = 0$, although essentially the same proof can be given for an arbitrary initial weight vector. In this case

$$\hat{W}_{k+1} = \hat{Y}_1 + \hat{Y}_2 + \cdots + \hat{Y}_k \qquad (5\cdot 10)$$

By hypothesis, there exists a solution vector, say W, such that $Y \cdot W > 0$ for all Y in $\mathcal{Y}'$. For a fixed solution vector W let

$$\min_{Y \in \mathcal{Y}'} Y \cdot W \triangleq a \qquad (5\cdot 11)$$

where $a > 0$. Taking the dot product of the solution vector W with both sides of Eq. (5·10) yields

$$\hat{W}_{k+1} \cdot W = \hat{Y}_1 \cdot W + \hat{Y}_2 \cdot W + \cdots + \hat{Y}_k \cdot W$$

Therefore, using Eq. (5·11) we have

$$\hat{W}_{k+1} \cdot W \geq ka \qquad (5\cdot 12)$$

The Cauchy-Schwarz inequality states that

$$|\hat{W}_{k+1}|^2 \geq \frac{(\hat{W}_{k+1} \cdot W)^2}{|W|^2} \qquad (5\cdot 13)$$

Using Eq. (5·12) in Eq. (5·13) and recalling that $a > 0$ we have

$$|\hat{W}_{k+1}|^2 \geq \frac{a^2}{|W|^2} k^2 \qquad (5\cdot 14)$$

Inequality (5·14) states that the squared length of the weight vector must grow at least quadratically with the number of steps.

Another line of reasoning will give us a contradictory bound. Since for all j

$$\hat{W}_{j+1} = \hat{W}_j + \hat{Y}_j \qquad (5\cdot 15)$$

we have
$$|\hat{\mathbf{W}}_{j+1}|^2 = |\hat{\mathbf{W}}_j|^2 + 2\hat{\mathbf{W}}_j \cdot \hat{\mathbf{Y}}_j + |\hat{\mathbf{Y}}_j|^2 \tag{5·16}$$

But $\hat{\mathbf{W}}_j \cdot \hat{\mathbf{Y}}_j \leq 0$; therefore
$$|\hat{\mathbf{W}}_{j+1}|^2 - |\hat{\mathbf{W}}_j|^2 \leq |\hat{\mathbf{Y}}_j|^2 \qquad \text{for all } j \tag{5·17}$$

We can add these inequalities for $j = 1, \ldots, k$ to obtain
$$|\hat{\mathbf{W}}_{k+1}|^2 \leq \sum_{j=1}^{k} |\hat{\mathbf{Y}}_j|^2 \tag{5·18}$$

If
$$M \triangleq \max_{\mathbf{Y} \in \mathcal{Y}} |\mathbf{Y}|^2 \tag{5·19}$$

then we can write
$$|\hat{\mathbf{W}}_{k+1}|^2 \leq kM \tag{5·20}$$

Inequality (5·20) states that the squared length of the weight vector can grow no faster than linearly with the number of changes made in the weight vector. Clearly, the bounds given by inequalities (5·14) and (5·20) conflict for sufficiently large values of k. Certainly k can be no larger than k_m, which is a solution to the equation

$$k_m M = \frac{k_m^2 a^2}{|\mathbf{W}|^2}$$

or
$$k_m = \frac{M|\mathbf{W}|^2}{a^2} \tag{5·21}$$

Therefore, we have proved (for $\hat{\mathbf{W}}_1 = 0$) that the fixed-increment error-correction procedure must terminate after at most k_m steps if a solution vector exists. (A similar proof can be given for arbitrary $\hat{\mathbf{W}}_1$.) But, since every pattern in $\mathcal{Y}$ occurs infinitely often in the training sequence, termination can occur only if a solution vector is found, which proves the theorem.

Other than the fact that a bound on the number of steps exists, thus proving the theorem, the bound itself is not very useful in estimating how many steps will be required in a given situation, since it depends on knowledge of a solution vector $\mathbf{W}$. It should also be pointed out that the bound on the number of steps will be different for the case of arbitrary $\hat{\mathbf{W}}_1$.

5·4 Proof 2

The following proof of Theorem 5·1 results from a simple geometric argument revealing that it is impossible to apply the fixed-increment error-correction procedure and remain forever outside the region of solution vectors.

Let $\mathcal{W}$ be the solution region of weight vectors satisfying inequality (5·6). That is,

$$\mathbf{W} \cdot \mathbf{Y} > 0 \qquad \text{for all } \mathbf{W} \text{ in } \mathcal{W} \text{ and each } \mathbf{Y} \text{ in } \mathcal{Y}'$$

Here $\mathcal{W}$ is an open convex region bounded by hyperplanes (the pattern hyperplanes) all of which pass through the origin. Such a region is called a convex *polyhedral cone* with vertex at the origin.

If a solution region $\mathcal{W}$ exists, then clearly each $\mathbf{W}$ in $\mathcal{W}$ can be scaled such that its dot product with each of the members of $\mathcal{Y}'$ is greater than any arbitrary positive constant. Let $\mathcal{W}'$ be the region of solution weight vectors, lying in the interior of $\mathcal{W}$, having the property that

$$\mathbf{W} \cdot \mathbf{Y} > \frac{(M+b)}{2} \qquad \text{for each } \mathbf{Y} \text{ in } \mathcal{Y}' \text{ and } \mathbf{W} \text{ in } \mathcal{W}' \qquad (5·22)$$

and for some given $b > 0$; $M = \max_{Y \in \mathcal{Y}} |\mathbf{Y}|^2$ as before.

The region $\mathcal{W}'$ is "insulated" from the boundaries of $\mathcal{W}$. The amount of insulation depends on M and b. By the remarks made in Chapter 4 in connection with the weight-space representation, it is clear that the boundaries of $\mathcal{W}'$ are hyperplanes parallel to the hyperplanes bounding $\mathcal{W}$. Specifically, if $\mathbf{W} \cdot \mathbf{Y} = 0$ bounds $\mathcal{W}$, then $\mathbf{W} \cdot \mathbf{Y} = \frac{1}{2}(M+b)$ bounds $\mathcal{W}'$. In this case these two parallel hyperplane boundaries are separated by a distance equal to $\frac{1}{2}(M+b)/(\mathbf{Y} \cdot \mathbf{Y})$. Because $\mathcal{W}'$ is bounded by hyperplanes, all parallel to those bounding $\mathcal{W}$, $\mathcal{W}'$ is also a convex polyhedral cone. Its vertex, however, is not at the origin but at some point whose distance from the origin increases with increasing M and b. A two-dimensional example is shown in Fig. 5·1.

Let $|\mathbf{W} - \hat{\mathbf{W}}_j|^2$ be the squared distance between some *fixed* interior point $\mathbf{W}$ in $\mathcal{W}'$ and $\hat{\mathbf{W}}_j$, where $\hat{\mathbf{W}}_j$ is the jth weight vector in the reduced weight-vector sequence $S_{\hat{W}}$. That is

$$|\mathbf{W} - \hat{\mathbf{W}}_j|^2 = \mathbf{W} \cdot \mathbf{W} - 2\mathbf{W} \cdot \hat{\mathbf{W}}_j + \hat{\mathbf{W}}_j \cdot \hat{\mathbf{W}}_j \qquad \text{for } j = 1, 2, \cdots \qquad (5·23)$$

86 TRAINING THEOREMS

We now compute the decrease in squared distance to $\mathbf{W}$, d_{k+1}, effected by the kth step

$$d_{k+1} = |\mathbf{W} - \hat{\mathbf{W}}_k|^2 - |\mathbf{W} - \hat{\mathbf{W}}_{k+1}|^2 \tag{5.24}$$

Let $\hat{\mathbf{Y}}_k$ be the kth pattern vector in the reduced training sequence $S\hat{y}$.

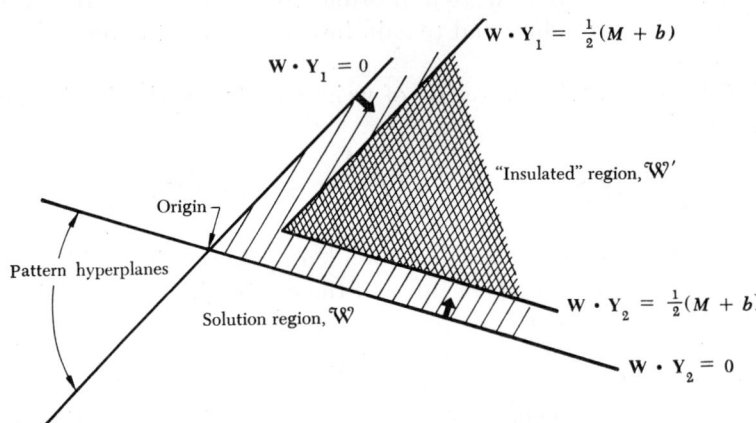

FIGURE 5·1 A solution region $\mathcal{W}$ and an insulated region $\mathcal{W}'$ as used in proof 2 of Theorem 5·1

Employing the fact that $\hat{\mathbf{W}}_{k+1} = \hat{\mathbf{W}}_k + \hat{\mathbf{Y}}_k$ and using Eq. (5·23) we then obtain

$$d_{k+1} = -2\hat{\mathbf{W}}_k \cdot \hat{\mathbf{Y}}_k + 2\mathbf{W} \cdot \hat{\mathbf{Y}}_k - \hat{\mathbf{Y}}_k \cdot \hat{\mathbf{Y}}_k \tag{5.25}$$

Since $\hat{\mathbf{W}}_k \cdot \hat{\mathbf{Y}}_k \leq 0$

$$d_{k+1} \geq 2\mathbf{W} \cdot \hat{\mathbf{Y}}_k - \hat{\mathbf{Y}}_k \cdot \hat{\mathbf{Y}}_k \geq 2\mathbf{W} \cdot \hat{\mathbf{Y}}_k - M$$

But, by inequality (5·22)

$$2\mathbf{W} \cdot \hat{\mathbf{Y}}_k - M > b \quad \text{for } \mathbf{W} \text{ in } \mathcal{W}' \tag{5.26}$$

Therefore

$$d_{k+1} > b > 0 \tag{5.27}$$

Inequality (5·27) states that the decrease in squared distance to some *fixed*, interior point in $\mathcal{W}'$ effected by any step must exceed a positive amount bounded away from zero. Because each pattern in $\mathcal{Y}$ occurs infinitely often in the training sequence, steps continue to be made until a weight vector in the solution region is attained, thus proving the theorem.

Some additional minor modifications can be made to the statement of Theorem 5·1 without affecting its validity. For example, we may seek a solution vector **W** with the property that

$$\mathbf{Y} \cdot \mathbf{W} > T \qquad \text{for each } \mathbf{Y} \in \mathcal{Y}_1$$

and

$$\mathbf{Y} \cdot \mathbf{W} < T \qquad \text{for each } \mathbf{Y} \in \mathcal{Y}_2$$

for some positive value of T. The proofs given above can easily be altered to show that the fixed-increment error-correction procedure, suitably modified by replacing zero by T in Eqs. (5·3) and (5·4), is still guaranteed to produce a solution weight vector when one exists.

5·5 A training theorem for R-category linear machines

Suppose we are given R finite subsets of augmented training pattern vectors $\mathcal{Y}_1, \mathcal{Y}_2, \ldots, \mathcal{Y}_R$. These subsets are *linearly separable* if and only if there exist R solution weight vectors $\mathbf{W}_1, \mathbf{W}_2, \ldots, \mathbf{W}_R$ such that

$$\mathbf{Y} \cdot \mathbf{W}_i > \mathbf{Y} \cdot \mathbf{W}_j \qquad \text{for each } \mathbf{Y} \in \mathcal{Y}_i \qquad i, j = 1, \ldots, R, i \neq j \qquad (5\cdot28)$$

If the subsets are linearly separable, then a *linear machine* exists which implements the desired classification of all members of the training subsets. The discriminant functions of the linear machine are given by

$$g_i(\mathbf{X}) = \mathbf{Y} \cdot \mathbf{W}_i \qquad i = 1, \ldots, R \qquad (5\cdot29)$$

We shall prove in this section that a generalization of the fixed-increment error-correction training procedure will produce a set of R solution weight vectors (and thus a set of R discriminant functions) for linearly separable training subsets.

We define a training sequence S_Y on the training set $\mathcal{Y} = \mathcal{Y}_1 \cup \mathcal{Y}_2 \cup \cdots \cup \mathcal{Y}_R$ as

$$S_Y = \mathbf{Y}_1, \mathbf{Y}_2, \ldots, \mathbf{Y}_k, \ldots \qquad (5\cdot30)$$

where each $\mathbf{Y}_k$ in S_Y is a member of one of the training subsets, and each member of each of the training subsets occurs infinitely often in S_Y. The *generalized* fixed-increment error-correction training procedure then recursively generates R sequences of weight vectors

$$\begin{aligned} S_{W_1} &= \mathbf{W}_1^{(1)}, \mathbf{W}_1^{(2)}, \ldots, \mathbf{W}_1^{(k)}, \ldots \\ &\cdots \\ S_{W_i} &= \mathbf{W}_i^{(1)}, \mathbf{W}_i^{(2)}, \ldots, \mathbf{W}_i^{(k)}, \ldots \\ &\cdots \\ S_{W_R} &= \mathbf{W}_R^{(1)}, \mathbf{W}_R^{(2)}, \ldots, \mathbf{W}_R^{(k)}, \ldots \end{aligned} \qquad (5\cdot31)$$

88   TRAINING THEOREMS

The rule for generating these sequences is as follows: $\mathbf{W}_1^{(1)}, \mathbf{W}_2^{(1)}, \ldots, \mathbf{W}_R^{(1)}$ are arbitrary initial weight vectors; $\mathbf{Y}_k$ belongs to one of the training subsets, say $\mathcal{Y}_i$.

Then, either

(a) $\mathbf{W}_i^{(k)} \cdot \mathbf{Y}_k > \mathbf{W}_j^{(k)} \cdot \mathbf{Y}_k \qquad j = 1, \ldots, R, j \neq i$

or

(b)   there exists some $l = 1, \ldots, R, l \neq i$ for which

$$\mathbf{W}_l^{(k)} \cdot \mathbf{Y}_k \geq \mathbf{W}_j^{(k)} \cdot \mathbf{Y}_k \qquad j = 1, \ldots, R, j \neq l$$

Under (a) we set

$$\mathbf{W}_j^{(k+1)} = \mathbf{W}_j^{(k)} \qquad \text{for all } j = 1, \ldots, R$$

Under (b) we set

$$\begin{aligned}\mathbf{W}_i^{(k+1)} &= \mathbf{W}_i^{(k)} + c\mathbf{Y}_k \\ \mathbf{W}_l^{(k+1)} &= \mathbf{W}_l^{(k)} - c\mathbf{Y}_k\end{aligned} \qquad (5\cdot 32)$$

and

$$\mathbf{W}_j^{(k+1)} = \mathbf{W}_j^{(k)} \qquad \text{for } j = 1, \ldots, R, j \neq i, j \neq l$$

where the correction increment c is a positive number.

After specifying a set of initial weight vectors, we can eliminate the occurrence of (a) by deleting from S_Y all pattern vectors for which (a) occurs. The resulting sequence $S_{\hat{Y}}$ will be called the *reduced training sequence*. The resulting weight-vector sequences $S_{\hat{W}_1}, S_{\hat{W}_2}, \ldots, S_{\hat{W}_R}$ generated from $S_{\hat{Y}}$ by the above rule will be called *reduced weight-vector sequences*. We can now state the following theorem.

Theorem 5·2

Let the training subsets $\mathcal{Y}_1, \mathcal{Y}_2, \ldots, \mathcal{Y}_R$ be linearly separable. Let $S_{W_1}, S_{W_2}, \ldots, S_{W_R}$ be the weight-vector sequences generated by any training sequence S_Y, using the generalized fixed-increment error-correction procedure and beginning with any initial weight vectors. Then, the weight-vector sequences will eventually produce a set of solution weight vectors. That is, for some set of indices $k_1, k_2, \ldots, k_R$, the set of vectors

$$\{\mathbf{W}_i^{(k_i)} = \mathbf{W}_i^{(k_i+1)} = \mathbf{W}_i^{(k_i+2)} = \cdots\} \qquad \text{for } i = 1, \ldots, R$$

will be a set of solution weight vectors.

Proof

The proof of Theorem 5·2 is accomplished by reformulating the R-category problem as a dichotomy problem in a higher-dimensional space and then applying Theorem 5·1. The first step is to generate a new set Z of higher-dimensional vectors from the training set y. Each vector $\mathbf{Z}$ in Z is of RD dimensions; it will be convenient to think of the RD dimensions of $\mathbf{Z}$ as being split into R blocks of D dimensions each. Each D-dimensional vector $\mathbf{Y}$ in y will generate $R - 1$ distinct RD-dimensional vectors in Z according to the following rules:

1. $\mathbf{Y}$ will belong to one of the training subsets; suppose it belongs to y_i.
2. We denote each of the $R - 1$ vectors in Z generated by $\mathbf{Y}$ by the symbol $\mathbf{Z}_i|_j(\mathbf{Y}), j = 1, \ldots, R, j \neq i$.
3. Let the ith block of D components of each $\mathbf{Z}_i|_j(\mathbf{Y})$ be set equal to $\mathbf{Y}$ for $j = 1, \ldots, R, j \neq i$.
4. For each $\mathbf{Z}_i|_j(\mathbf{Y}), j = 1, \ldots, R, j \neq i$, let the jth block of D components be set equal to $-\mathbf{Y}$.
5. Let all other components of each $\mathbf{Z}_i|_j(\mathbf{Y})$ be set equal to zero.

The above construction is illustrated by the following example. Let $\mathbf{Y} = (y_1, y_2, y_3)$ be a member of y_3, and let $R = 4$. Then the three vectors $\mathbf{Z}_3|_1(\mathbf{Y}), \mathbf{Z}_3|_2(\mathbf{Y})$, and $\mathbf{Z}_3|_4(\mathbf{Y})$ are

$$\mathbf{Z}_3|_1(\mathbf{Y}) = (-y_1, -y_2, -y_3, 0, 0, 0, y_1, y_2, y_3, 0, 0, 0)$$
$$\mathbf{Z}_3|_2(\mathbf{Y}) = (0, 0, 0, -y_1, -y_2, -y_3, y_1, y_2, y_3, 0, 0, 0)$$
$$\mathbf{Z}_3|_4(\mathbf{Y}) = (0, 0, 0, 0, 0, 0, y_1, y_2, y_3, -y_1, -y_2, -y_3)$$

The subsets $y_1, y_2, \ldots, y_R$ are *linearly separable* if and only if the set Z is linearly contained. To verify this statement, suppose that $y_1, y_2, \ldots, y_R$ are linearly separable with a set of solution weight vectors $\mathbf{W}_1, \mathbf{W}_2, \ldots, \mathbf{W}_R$; then observe that Z is linearly contained with an RD-dimensional vector $\mathbf{V} = (\mathbf{W}_1, \mathbf{W}_2, \ldots, \mathbf{W}_R)$. Conversely, suppose that Z is linearly contained with an RD-dimensional vector $\mathbf{V}$. This vector can be partitioned to yield the solution weight vectors $\mathbf{W}_1, \mathbf{W}_2, \ldots, \mathbf{W}_R$.

The next step in the proof is to form from the reduced training sequence $S_{\hat{Y}}$ and the reduced weight-vector sequences $S_{\hat{W}_1}, \ldots, S_{\hat{W}_R}$ a corresponding sequence of vectors from the set Z. Let us denote this sequence of vectors from Z by the symbol S_Z. Corresponding to the kth member, $\hat{Y}_k$ of $S_{\hat{Y}}$ is a vector $\mathbf{Z}_k$ in S_Z. We determine $\mathbf{Z}_k$ as follows: Suppose that $\hat{Y}_k$ belongs to y_i. Because $\hat{Y}_k$ is a member of the *reduced* training sequence we know that there exists some $l \neq i$ such that $\hat{\mathbf{W}}_l^{(k)} \cdot \hat{\mathbf{Y}}_k \geq \hat{\mathbf{W}}_j^{(k)} \cdot \hat{\mathbf{Y}}_k$ for all $j = 1, \ldots, R, j \neq l$. That is, the kth pattern in $S_{\hat{Y}}$ is inaccurately classified as a member of $\mathcal{Y}_l$ when it actually belongs to $\mathcal{Y}_i$; $\mathbf{Z}_k$ is then expressed by

$$\mathbf{Z}_k = \mathbf{Z}_{i|l}(\hat{\mathbf{Y}}_k) \tag{5.33}$$

That is, $\mathbf{Z}_k$ is a vector whose ith block of D components is set equal to $\hat{\mathbf{Y}}_k$, whose lth block of D components is set equal to $-\hat{\mathbf{Y}}_k$, and whose other components are all equal to zero. We apply this rule to each element of $S_{\hat{Y}}$ to generate the sequence S_Z.

The final step of the proof is to form a sequence S_V of RD-dimensional weight vectors from the reduced weight-vector sequences, $S_{\hat{W}_1}, \ldots, S_{\hat{W}_R}$. Let $\mathbf{V}_k$ be the kth member of the sequence S_V. If the respective kth members of $S_{\hat{W}_1}, \ldots, S_{\hat{W}_R}$ are given by $\hat{\mathbf{W}}_1^{(k)}, \ldots, \hat{\mathbf{W}}_R^{(k)}$ then $\mathbf{V}_k$ is determined as follows: The first block of D components of $\mathbf{V}_k$ is given by the components of $\hat{\mathbf{W}}_1^{(k)}$, the second block of D components of $\mathbf{V}_k$ is given by the components of $\hat{\mathbf{W}}_2^{(k)}$, etc. That is

$$\mathbf{V}_k = [\hat{\mathbf{W}}_1^{(k)}, \hat{\mathbf{W}}_2^{(k)}, \ldots, \hat{\mathbf{W}}_R^{(k)}] \tag{5.34}$$

Note that the same sequence S_V could have been obtained by applying the ordinary (two-category) fixed-increment error-correction procedure using the sequence S_Z and starting with an initial weight vector $\mathbf{V}_1 = [\hat{\mathbf{W}}_1^{(1)}, \hat{\mathbf{W}}_2^{(1)}, \ldots, \hat{\mathbf{W}}_R^{(1)}]$. The sequence S_Z can be regarded as a reduced training sequence of the patterns in $\mathcal{Z}$, and since $\mathcal{Z}$ is linearly contained, the application of the fixed-increment procedure must result, by Theorem 5·1, in a solution weight vector. Therefore, the sequence S_V must terminate, meaning that the reduced weight-vector sequences $S_{\hat{W}_1}, \ldots, S_{\hat{W}_R}$ must also terminate. But these sequences can only terminate when a set of solution weight vectors satisfying Eq. (5·28) is found, thus proving the theorem.

5·6 A related training theorem for the case $R = 2$

In Chapter 4 we discussed another error-correction procedure, the fractional correction rule. In this rule the correction increment at the kth step c_k is set equal to that value which will move the weight vector a desired fraction of the way toward the pattern plane. This fraction we call λ.

Let us consider again the adjusted training set $\mathcal{Y}'$ composed of the union of $\mathcal{Y}_1$ (the augmented training patterns belonging to category 1)

TRAINING THEOREMS

and $\mathcal{Y}_2'$ (the negatives of the augmented training patterns belonging to category 2). We desire to find a solution weight vector $\mathbf{W}$ such that

$$\mathbf{W} \cdot \mathbf{Y} > 0$$

for each $\mathbf{Y}$ in $\mathcal{Y}'$. Let $\mathcal{W}$ be the set of solution weight vectors. As before, $\mathcal{W}$ is an open convex polyhedral cone.

Let $S_{Y'} = \mathbf{Y}_1', \mathbf{Y}_2', \ldots, \mathbf{Y}_k', \ldots$ be a training sequence on $\mathcal{Y}'$. The fractional correction rule generates a weight-vector sequence S_W as follows:

Begin with any arbitrary weight vector $\mathbf{W}_1$.
Then, for $k = 1, 2, \ldots$,

$$\begin{aligned} \mathbf{W}_{k+1} &= \mathbf{W}_k + \lambda \frac{|\mathbf{W}_k \cdot \mathbf{Y}_k'|}{\mathbf{Y}_k' \cdot \mathbf{Y}_k'} \mathbf{Y}_k' && \text{if } \mathbf{Y}_k' \cdot \mathbf{W}_k \leq 0 \\ \mathbf{W}_{k+1} &= \mathbf{W}_k && \text{if } \mathbf{Y}_k' \cdot \mathbf{W}_k > 0 \end{aligned} \quad (5.35)$$

We note that the value of the correction increment is given by

$$c_k = \lambda \frac{|\mathbf{W}_k \cdot \mathbf{Y}_k'|}{\mathbf{Y}_k' \cdot \mathbf{Y}_k'} \quad (5.36)$$

After specifying an initial weight vector $\mathbf{W}_1$ we may remove from the training sequence those patterns $\mathbf{Y}_k'$ for which $\mathbf{W}_k \cdot \mathbf{Y}_k' > 0$. The reduced training sequence $S_{\hat{Y}}$ then creates a reduced weight-vector sequence $S_{\hat{W}}$ such that

$$\hat{\mathbf{Y}}_k \cdot \hat{\mathbf{W}}_k \leq 0 \quad (5.37)$$

for all $\hat{\mathbf{Y}}_k$ in $S_{\hat{Y}}$ and for all $\hat{\mathbf{W}}_k$ in $S_{\hat{W}}$.

Theorem 5·3

Let $\mathcal{Y}'$ be a set of linearly contained patterns. Let $S_{\hat{W}}$ be the reduced weight-vector sequence generated by any reduced training sequence $S_{\hat{Y}}$, using the fractional correction rule and beginning with any initial weight vector $\hat{\mathbf{W}}_1$. Then for $0 < \lambda \leq 2$, either $S_{\hat{W}}$ *terminates* in $\mathcal{W}$ or on its boundary, or $\hat{\mathbf{W}}_k$ *converges* to a point on the boundary of $\mathcal{W}$.

Proof

We assume that $S_{\hat{W}}$ is an infinite sequence, since if it were otherwise it would terminate. Let $\mathbf{W}$ be any fixed point in $\mathcal{W}$. It is easy to verify

92 TRAINING THEOREMS

that if $0 < \lambda \leq 2$, then

$$|\hat{\mathbf{W}}_{k+1} - \mathbf{W}| \leq |\hat{\mathbf{W}}_k - \mathbf{W}| \qquad (5\cdot 38)$$

for *all* $\mathbf{W}$ in $\mathcal{W}$. We therefore say that $\hat{\mathbf{W}}_{k+1}$ is *pointwise closer* than $\hat{\mathbf{W}}_k$ to $\mathcal{W}$. As a first step in proving the theorem, we shall show that the sequence $S_{\hat{W}}$ converges to a point $\mathbf{P}$.

For any fixed $\mathbf{W}$ in $\mathcal{W}$ let $\lim_{k \to \infty} |\hat{\mathbf{W}}_k - \mathbf{W}| = l(\mathbf{W})$; $l(\mathbf{W})$ exists since Eq. (5·38) holds for all k. We conclude that $\hat{\mathbf{W}}_k$ must converge to a hypersphere $S(\mathbf{W})$, centered at $\mathbf{W}$ and with some radius $l(\mathbf{W})$. But the preceding statement is true for all $\mathbf{W}$ in $\mathcal{W}$. Therefore, $\hat{\mathbf{W}}_k$ must converge to one of the points defined by the joint intersection of all hyperspheres $S(\mathbf{W})$ for all $\mathbf{W}$ in $\mathcal{W}$.

We next demonstrate that there can be only one such point $\mathbf{P}$ of joint intersection. Suppose there were at least two distinct points $\mathbf{P}$ and $\mathbf{P}'$. Let H be the hyperplane of points equidistant from $\mathbf{P}$ and $\mathbf{P}'$. For $\mathbf{W}$ in $\mathcal{W}$, $S(\mathbf{W})$ must contain both $\mathbf{P}$ and $\mathbf{P}'$ and therefore $\mathbf{W}$ must lie in H. We conclude that $\mathcal{W}$ must also be in H contrary to the fact that $\mathcal{W}$ is the interior of an open polyhedral cone. Therefore the sequence $S_{\hat{W}}$ converges to a single point.

We next show that this point $\mathbf{P}$ must be on the boundary of $\mathcal{W}$. Suppose it is not, but instead lies outside* at a distance Δ from one of the pattern hyperplanes bounding $\mathcal{W}$. But the pattern corresponding to this hyperplane will eventually occur in $S_{\hat{Y}}$, say at the kth step. Suppose k to be sufficiently large that $\hat{\mathbf{W}}_k$ is separated from the limit point $\mathbf{P}$ by a distance less than $\epsilon < \Delta$.

For any $\lambda > 0$, if $\Delta > 0$, we can choose ϵ small enough (by choosing k large enough) such that $\hat{\mathbf{W}}_{k+1}$ will be at a distance greater than ϵ from $\mathbf{P}$, contradicting the assumption that $\mathbf{P}$ is a limit point. Therefore, the sequence $S_{\hat{W}}$ must converge to a point on the boundary of $\mathcal{W}$, proving the theorem.

5·7 Bibliographical and historical remarks

The first proof of Theorem 5·1 was outlined by Rosenblatt.[1] Subsequent proofs have been given by Joseph,[2] Block,[3] Charnes,[4] Novikoff,[5] Singleton,[6] Ridgway,[7] and possibly others. Our Proof 1 follows the method

---

* Since $S_{\hat{W}}$ terminates when $\hat{\mathbf{W}}_k$ is in $\mathcal{W}$ for some k, the limit point $\mathbf{P}$ cannot be inside $\mathcal{W}$.

developed by Novikoff[5] and Singleton.[6] Proof 2 is an adaptation of the one given by Ridgway.[7] Block[3] has proved a generalized version of Theorem 5·1 in which the correction increment c_k of Eq. (5·4) need not be independent of k.

Theorem 5·2 was first proved by C. Kesler at Cornell University. Our proof is a version of Kesler's as it was related to the author during discussions in July, 1963.

Theorem 5·3 is a slightly modified version of a theorem by Motzkin and Schoenberg.[8] In their theorem, Motzkin and Schoenberg specified a training sequence which is generated recursively from the weight-vector sequence. The $(k + 1)$th pattern in the training sequence is that member of $\mathcal{Y}'$ which has the smallest (most-negative) dot product with $\mathbf{W}_{k+1}$. They also show that for this training sequence and for $\lambda = 2$, the reduced weight-vector sequence is guaranteed to *terminate*, providing, of course, that $\mathcal{W}$ is nonempty. Using this same training sequence, Agmon[9] proved that the rate of convergence of the weight-vector sequence is geometric. R. Duda of the Stanford Research Institute has observed that the reduced weight-vector sequence actually either terminates or converges for *any* training sequence if $0 < \lambda \leq 2$, hence our Theorem 5·3. Duda also pointed out that the reduced weight-vector sequence is guaranteed to terminate for *any* training sequence if $\lambda = 2$.

REFERENCES

1. Rosenblatt, F.: On the Convergence of Reinforcement Procedures in Simple Perceptrons, *Cornell Aeronautical Laboratory Report VG-1196-G-4*, Buffalo, New York, February, 1960.
2. Joseph, R. D.: Contributions to Perceptron Theory, *Cornell Aeronautical Laboratory Report VG-1196-G-7*, Buffalo, New York, June, 1960.
3. Block, H. D.: The Perceptron: A Model for Brain Functioning, I, *Reviews of Modern Physics*, vol. 34, pp. 123–135, January, 1962.
4. Charnes, A.: On Some Fundamental Theorems of Perceptron Theory and Their Geometry, in J. Tou and R. Wilcox (eds.), "Computer and Information Sciences," Spartan Books, Washington, D.C., 1964.
5. Novikoff, A. B. J.: On Convergence Proofs for Perceptrons, *Stanford Research Institute Report*, prepared for the Office of Naval Research under Contract Nonr 3438(00), January, 1963.
6. Singleton, R. C.: A Test for Linear Separability as Applied to Self-organizing Machines, in Yovits, Jacobi, and Goldstein (eds.), "Self-organizing Systems —1962," pp. 503–524, Spartan Books, Washington, D.C., 1962.

7 Ridgway, W. C.: An Adaptive Logic System with Generalizing Properties, *Stanford Electronics Laboratories Technical Report* 1556-1, prepared under Air Force Contract AF 33(616)-7726, Stanford University, Stanford, California, April, 1962.
8 Motzkin, T. S., and I. J. Schoenberg: The Relaxation Method for Linear Inequalities, *Canadian Journal of Mathematics*, vol. 6, no. 3, pp. 393–404, 1954.
9 Agmon, S.: The Relaxation Method for Linear Inequalities, *Canadian Journal of Mathematics*, vol. 6, no. 3, pp. 382–392, 1954.

CHAPTER 6

LAYERED MACHINES

6·1 Layered networks of TLUs

Networks of interconnected TLUs have often been proposed as pattern-classifying machines. In these networks the binary responses of some TLUs are used as inputs to other TLUs. If $R = 2$, the binary output of one of the TLUs is taken to be the response of the whole machine. Figure 6·1 is an example of such a network.

The properties of TLU networks are not yet fully understood. (For example, expressions do not yet exist for the capacity of these networks nor training theorems for them.) Nevertheless, it is believed that these networks would make useful pattern classifiers because of the complex decision surfaces that they can implement.

In this chapter, we shall investigate a special class of networks, called *layered machines*, about which some understanding and experience have already been obtained. We shall limit our discussion primarily to the case $R = 2$. A layered machine is a network of TLUs organized in

96 LAYERED MACHINES

layers (see Fig. 6·2). Each TLU in the first layer has as its inputs the pattern to be classified. The outputs of the first layer of TLUs are used as the inputs to the second layer of TLUs, and so on. The TLUs in the second and subsequent layers have as their inputs the outputs of the

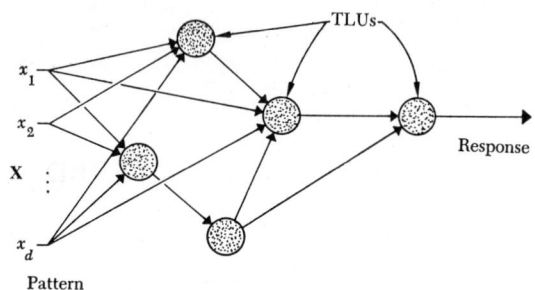

FIGURE 6·1 A network of TLUs

TLUs in the preceding layer only. The output of the single TLU in the final layer is the response of the machine.

Layered machines can implement quite complex decision surfaces. We shall see later in this chapter that the decison surfaces of layered machines can be obtained by piecewise linear discriminant functions. So

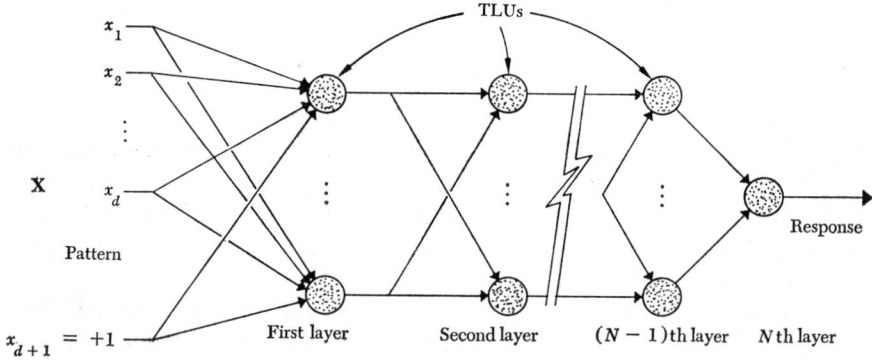

FIGURE 6·2 A layered machine

far, our study of trainable pattern-classifying machines has been concerned only with discriminant functions which are members of Φ function families. Since piecewise linear discriminant functions are not Φ functions, the training methods that we have already discussed cannot be directly applied to layered machines.

LAYERED MACHINES

In general, layered machines can be trained by varying the weights associated with *each* TLU in the network. There do not yet exist, however, efficient adjustment rules for such thorough training of a layered machine. In the next three sections, we shall discuss a method in which only the TLUs in one layer of the network are trained.

6·2   Committee machines

Suppose we have training subsets $\mathcal{Y}_1$ and $\mathcal{Y}_2$ of augmented training patterns which are *not* linearly separable. That is, no vector **W** exists such that

and
$$\mathbf{Y} \cdot \mathbf{W} > 0 \quad \text{for each } \mathbf{Y} \text{ in } \mathcal{Y}_1$$
$$\mathbf{Y} \cdot \mathbf{W} < 0 \quad \text{for each } \mathbf{Y} \text{ in } \mathcal{Y}_2 \quad (6\cdot 1)$$

Therefore, it would be impossible to train a single TLU to dichotomize the training set correctly. Perhaps some more complex machine, for example a layered machine, might be capable of being trained to dichotomize the training set correctly. We shall study in this section a special case of a layered machine called a *committee machine*.

Consider the three pattern hyperplanes (lines) in Fig. 6·3 for the case $D = d + 1 = 2$. The arrows attached to the lines point toward the positive sides of the lines. These lines divide the weight space into six regions; thus, there are six linear dichotomies of three one-dimensional patterns. But there are $2^3 = 8$ different possible dichotomies of three patterns; therefore two of the dichotomies are not linear. As an example of a nonlinear dichotomy, consider the one given by the subsets

$$\begin{aligned}\mathcal{Y}_1 &= \{\mathbf{Y}_1, \mathbf{Y}_2\} \\ \mathcal{Y}_2 &= \mathbf{Y}_3\end{aligned} \quad (6\cdot 2)$$

None of the regions formed by these three pattern hyperplanes contains a weight vector **W** for which

and
$$\begin{aligned}\mathbf{Y}_1 \cdot \mathbf{W} &> 0 \\ \mathbf{Y}_2 \cdot \mathbf{W} &> 0 \quad \text{indicating category-1 responses} \\ \mathbf{Y}_3 \cdot \mathbf{W} &< 0 \quad \text{indicating a category-2 response}\end{aligned} \quad (6\cdot 3)$$

98 LAYERED MACHINES

But consider the "committee" of weight vectors $\mathbf{W}_1$, $\mathbf{W}_2$, and $\mathbf{W}_3$ in Fig. 6·3. With respect to these weight vectors, we have the inequalities

$$\begin{array}{lll} \mathbf{W}_1 \cdot \mathbf{Y}_1 > 0 & \mathbf{W}_1 \cdot \mathbf{Y}_2 > 0 & \mathbf{W}_1 \cdot \mathbf{Y}_3 > 0 \\ \mathbf{W}_2 \cdot \mathbf{Y}_1 < 0 & \mathbf{W}_2 \cdot \mathbf{Y}_2 > 0 & \mathbf{W}_2 \cdot \mathbf{Y}_3 < 0 \\ \mathbf{W}_3 \cdot \mathbf{Y}_1 > 0 & \mathbf{W}_3 \cdot \mathbf{Y}_2 < 0 & \mathbf{W}_3 \cdot \mathbf{Y}_3 < 0 \end{array} \quad (6\cdot 4)$$

We note that for each of the three patterns the *majority* of the weight vectors yield dot products having the correct sign. Therefore these three weight vectors can be employed by a *committee* of three TLUs in such a

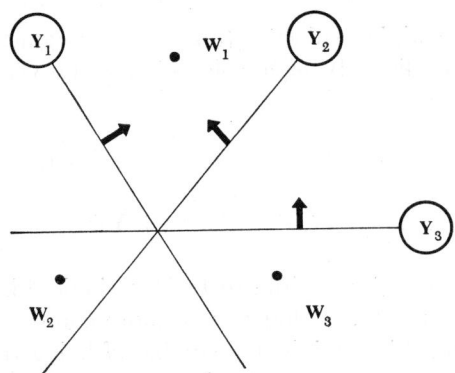

FIGURE 6·3 A commmittee of weight vectors

way that the consensus or majority of the TLU responses is correct for each pattern. The consensus can be polled by an additional *vote-taking* TLU which sums the binary outputs of the three committee TLUs and compares this sum against a threshold of zero. We shall call the complete network of TLUs a *committee machine*.

In general, a committee machine could have P committee TLUs with weight vectors $\mathbf{W}_1, \ldots, \mathbf{W}_P$, where P is odd. Such a machine is said to be of *size P*. These P committee TLUs comprise the first layer of a two-layer machine. The second layer consists of the vote-taking TLU whose response is the majority response of the committee TLUs. A committee machine of size P is depicted in Fig. 6·4.

The committee machine can be generalized by allowing the committee TLUs to have different voting strengths. A further modification consists of setting the vote-taking TLU threshold to a value that would require other than a simple majority of committee TLU responses of $+1$ in order that the machine response be $+1$. The possibility of such variants of the committee machine increases its classifying power but, un-

LAYERED MACHINES

fortunately, no efficient training procedures are known which simultaneously locate the weight vectors and adjust their voting strengths. Therefore, our discussion will concentrate on the "simple-majority" committee machine with a fixed vote-taking TLU.

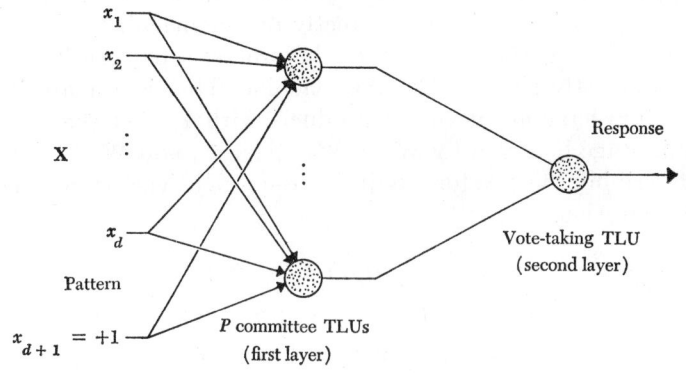

FIGURE 6·4   A committee machine

6·3   A training procedure for committee machines

Suppose that we have training pattern subsets $\mathcal{Y}_1$ and $\mathcal{Y}_2$, comprising the training set $\mathcal{Y}$, and we wish to find a committee machine of size P to separate these subsets. To accomplish this, we must locate P weight vectors such that the majority of them are on the correct side of every pattern hyperplane.

There do not yet exist any training theorems for committee machines parallel to those given in Chapter 5 for Φ machines. There does exist, however, a training procedure which has proven satisfactory in a variety of different experiments. This procedure is usually successful in locating the P weight vectors if, indeed, P weight vectors exist which will separate the two training subsets. In some contrived situations the procedure does not always terminate successfully, but even for these, success can usually be obtained if the size of the machine is made slightly larger than the minimum required theoretically.

The training procedure iteratively adjusts P weight vectors until they successfully dichotomize the training set $\mathcal{Y}$. For reasons to be made clear later, it is necessary that the lengths of the initial weight vectors all be approximately the same. Often each of the initial weight vectors is taken to have zero components. The patterns are arranged in a training sequence and presented to the machine, one at a time, for trial. The procedure is similar to the error-correction methods previously described, in that adjustments to the weight vectors are made *only* when a pattern in the training set is classified incorrectly by the machine.

Suppose that at the kth stage of the process a pattern $\mathbf{Y}_k$, belonging to $\mathcal{Y}_1$, is incorrectly classified by the machine. That is, a majority of the weight vectors have negative dot products with $\mathbf{Y}_k$. Let the weight vectors at this stage be given by $\mathbf{W}_1^{(k)}, \mathbf{W}_2^{(k)}, \ldots,$ and $\mathbf{W}_P^{(k)}$.

In describing the rule for modifying the weight vectors we shall make use of the notation

$$N_k = \sum_{j=1}^{P} \text{sgn}\,(\mathbf{W}_j^{(k)} \cdot \mathbf{Y}_k) \qquad (6\cdot 5)$$

where

$$\begin{aligned}\text{sgn}\,a &= +1 \quad \text{if } a \geq 0 \\ &= -1 \quad \text{if } a < 0\end{aligned} \qquad (6\cdot 6)$$

The expression N_k is the number of weight vectors at the kth stage having a nonnegative dot product with $\mathbf{Y}_k$ minus the number having a negative dot product with $\mathbf{Y}_k$.* Thus, N_k is the sum operated on by the threshold of the vote-taking TLU. If the majority of the vectors $\mathbf{W}_1^{(k)}, \ldots, \mathbf{W}_j^{(k)}, \ldots, \mathbf{W}_P^{(k)}$ have nonnegative dot products with the vector $\mathbf{Y}_k$, then N_k will be greater than zero and the machine response will be $+1$. Since P is odd, N_k can never equal zero or be even.

We have assumed that at the kth stage of the process the pattern $\mathbf{Y}_k$, belonging to category 1, is incorrectly classified. In this case $N_k < 0$. Since N_k cannot be even it follows that exactly $(P - N_k)/2$ of the P committee TLUs have negative responses. If the responses of at least $\frac{1}{2}(|N_k| + 1)$ of these negatively responding TLUs were changed from -1 to $+1$, then the majority of the committee TLUs would have positive responses, and the machine would respond correctly to $\mathbf{Y}_k$. For example, if exactly seven TLUs in a committee of size nine had negative responses to $\mathbf{Y}_k$, then $N_k = -5$. At least three of the seven TLUs with negative responses would have to be changed in order that the majority of the committee have positive responses.

The committee training procedure calls for the adjustment of the minimum number of TLUs needed to correct the machine response. The

---

* For simplicity of explanation in describing the operation of a committee machine we assume that a dot product equal to zero causes the same TLU response as does a positive dot product. That is, a weight vector lying *on* a pattern hyperplane is assumed to be on the positive side. Other conventions could also have been adopted.

weight vectors which are adjusted are those which have dot products closest to zero. (Ties are resolved arbitrarily.) These, in one sense, are the *easiest* to adjust. The adjustment is achieved by the familiar process of adding (or subtracting) the pattern vector to (or from) the weight vector.

Thus, if $\mathbf{Y}_k$ causes a majority of the committee TLUs to respond negatively, we adjust the $\frac{1}{2}(|N_k| + 1)$ weight vectors making the least-negative (but not positive) dot products with $\mathbf{Y}_k$. If the weight vector $\mathbf{W}_j^{(k)}$ is among this set of $\frac{1}{2}(|N_k| + 1)$ weight vectors, it is adjusted by the rule

$$\mathbf{W}_j^{(k+1)} = \mathbf{W}_j^{(k)} + c_j^{(k)} \mathbf{Y}_k \qquad (6\cdot 7)$$

where $c_j^{(k)}$ is the correction increment which we take to be positive. All the other $P - \frac{1}{2}(|N_k| + 1)$ weight vectors are left unaltered at this stage.

If at the kth stage the machine incorrectly classifies a pattern belonging to $\mathcal{Y}_2$, a corresponding rule is used to adjust $\frac{1}{2}(|N_k| + 1)$ of the $(P + N_k)/2$ weight vectors making nonnegative dot products with $\mathbf{Y}_k$. Those $\frac{1}{2}(|N_k| + 1)$ having the least-positive (but not negative) dot products are adjusted by the rule

$$\mathbf{W}_j^{(k+1)} = \mathbf{W}_j^{(k)} - c_j^{(k)} \mathbf{Y}_k \qquad (6\cdot 8)$$

where $c_j^{(k)}$ is a positive correction increment and all other $P - \frac{1}{2}(|N_k| + 1)$ weight vectors are left unadjusted.

The correction increments $c_j^{(k)}$ can be fixed, positive constants, independent of j and k, analogous to the fixed-increment correction rule, or they may be chosen for each k and j large enough to effect a reversal of the sign of N_k.

A simpler description of this training procedure is permitted if the subset $\mathcal{Y}_2$ is replaced by $\mathcal{Y}_2'$, in which each member is the negative of the corresponding member of $\mathcal{Y}_2$. Since we now desire that N_k be positive for each k, Eq. (6·7) describes the adjustments, if any, to be made at any stage. In Sec. 6·4 we will illustrate this training procedure for an example in which we have three augmented patterns of two dimensions.

6·4 An example

The training procedure described above can be illustrated quite clearly by a two-dimensional example. The geometrical interpretation of this training procedure is quite simply explained: When the majority of the weight vectors are on the negative side of a pattern hyperplane, only

102 LAYERED MACHINES

those that are *closest* to this pattern hyperplane are adjusted by the addition of the pattern vector. Consider the three pattern vectors and their corresponding pattern hyperplanes (lines) shown in Fig. 6·5. The arrows indicate the positive sides of the lines. In this figure is shown the history of weight-vector adjustments produced by presenting the patterns in the order $Y_1, Y_2, Y_3, Y_1, Y_2, Y_3, Y_1, Y_2, Y_3, \ldots$ for a committee machine of size three. Suppose that we desire to find a set of weight vectors having

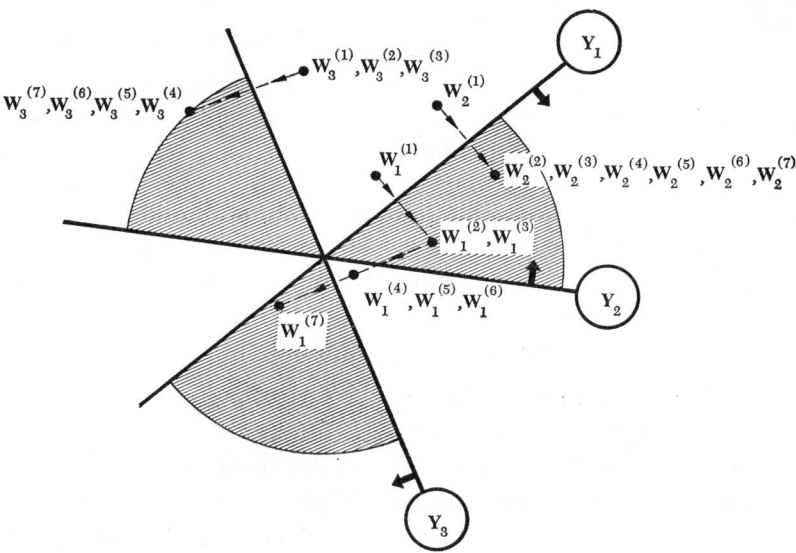

FIGURE 6·5 An example illustrating the committee training procedure

the property that the majority make positive dot products with each of the pattern vectors Y_1, Y_2, Y_3; then, adjustments to the weight vector(s) are made whenever $N_k < 0$. (The reader could assume, for example, that $\mathcal{Y}_1$ contains Y_2 and that $\mathcal{Y}_2$ contains $-Y_1$ and $-Y_3$.)

The successive weight vectors are indicated by points and the appropriate labels $W_j^{(k)}$ adjacent to them. The shaded regions indicate those regions that must each contain one of the weight vectors before the process can successfully terminate in the correct classification of the patterns in the training set.

The initial weight vectors are chosen arbitrarily as shown. At the first stage, when we are examining the positions of the initial weight vectors with respect to the pattern hyperplane corresponding to Y_1, we see that all of them (hence, the majority) are on the incorrect side. This situation calls for the adjustment of two of them, and $W_1^{(1)}$ and $W_2^{(1)}$

are adjusted as shown since they are the closest to the Y_1 pattern hyperplane (they make the two least-negative dot products with Y_1). At the next stage, examining the weight-vector positions with respect to the Y_2 pattern hyperplane we see that all of them (hence, again, the majority) are on the correct side; thus, no adjustments are made. For Y_3, we again adjust two weight vectors. Later, another adjustment for Y_3 results in a satisfactory location of the three committee weight vectors. At this stage the training process terminates.

This example can also be used to illustrate the necessity for beginning with initial weight vectors of approximately the same length. Suppose that $W_2^{(1)}$ were many times longer (in the same direction) than is shown in Fig. 6·5. If it were made too long, it would never be among the weight vectors closest to the hyperplanes which it must eventually cross. Therefore, it would never be adjusted, and W_1 and W_3 would wander around perpetually in a futile search for stable locations, which do not exist so long as W_2 cannot cooperate by leaving its initial region.* This same phenomenon accounts for instances in which the committee training procedure does not converge even when the initial weight vectors are all of the same length. Occasionally one of the weight vectors wanders off too far and is consequently never adjusted again. The other weight vectors are then left to seek a solution that they alone cannot achieve. Such a situation is usually avoided if the number of committee weight vectors is larger than the theoretical minimum.

6·5 Transformation properties of layered machines

We have seen in Secs. 6·2 to 6·4 that the concept of the first-layer TLUs as voters in a "committee" is a productive representation for two-layer machines. Another representation, to be discussed in this section, concentrates on the nonlinear transformations implemented by each layer of TLUs.

Consider the layered machine shown in Fig. 6·2. The binary outputs of the first layer of TLUs can be regarded as the components of a vector. If there are P_1 TLUs in the first layer, these TLUs transform the d-dimensional input pattern vector into a P_1-dimensional vector with binary com-

* A theorem appearing in a report by Efron[7] shows that the lengths of W_1 and W_3 remain bounded during the error-correction procedure, thus guaranteeing that neither of them can stray farther from any of the pattern hyperplanes than the initial (large) distance between W_2 and the pattern hyperplanes.

ponents of $+1$ and -1. Thus, each point in the pattern space is transformed into one of the vertices of a P_1-dimensional hypercube. This hypercube we shall call the *first image space* or the I_1 space. The transformation between the pattern space and the I_1 space depends on the values of the weights in the first layer. For a given set of weights, the first layer will transform a finite set $\mathfrak{X}$ of pattern vectors into a finite set $\mathcal{J}^{(1)}$ of image-space vertices.

Now looking at the second layer of TLUs, we can say that it transforms the vertices of I_1 space into a *second image space* or I_2 space. If there are P_2 TLUs in the second layer, these TLUs transform each of the I_1-space vertices into one of the vertices of a P_2-dimensional hypercube. The transformation from I_1 space to I_2 space depends on the values of the weights in the second layer. For a given set of weights, the second layer will transform a set $\mathcal{J}^{(1)}$ of P_1-dimensional image-space vertices into a finite set $\mathcal{J}^{(2)}$ of P_2-dimensional image-space vertices.

Such a transformation occurs at each layer until the TLU in the last or Nth layer transforms the set $\mathcal{J}^{(N-1)}$ of image points into the two vertices of a one-dimensional cube. These two vertices represent the two possible responses of the layered machine. Thus the sequence of transformations acting on a set $\mathfrak{X}$ of pattern vectors yields intermediate sets $\mathcal{J}^{(1)}, \mathcal{J}^{(2)}, \ldots, \mathcal{J}^{(N-1)}$ and finally results in the set of two points in a one-dimensional space.

The action of a layered machine in dichotomizing two pattern subsets $\mathfrak{X}_1$ and $\mathfrak{X}_2$ can then be described as follows. The first layer transforms $\mathfrak{X}_1$ and $\mathfrak{X}_2$ into $\mathcal{J}_1^{(1)}$ and $\mathcal{J}_2^{(1)}$, respectively. The second layer transforms $\mathcal{J}_1^{(1)}$ and $\mathcal{J}_2^{(1)}$ into $\mathcal{J}_1^{(2)}$ and $\mathcal{J}_2^{(2)}$, respectively, and so on, until finally the $(N-1)$th layer produces two *linearly separable* subsets $\mathcal{J}_1^{(N-1)}$ and $\mathcal{J}_2^{(N-1)}$. Then and only then can the single TLU in the Nth layer produce the desired responses for each of the patterns in $\mathfrak{X}_1$ and $\mathfrak{X}_2$.

Given training subsets $\mathfrak{X}_1$ and $\mathfrak{X}_2$, the training problem for layered machines can then be viewed as a problem of adjusting the various layers of weights such that the transformations implemented by the first $N-1$ layers result in linearly separable subsets at the $(N-1)$th layer. Training the TLU in the final layer can then be accomplished by one of the error-correction methods discussed in Chapter 4.

Let us illustrate the above ideas with an example using three-dimensional patterns. Since each TLU implements a linear separating surface, its response for any given three-dimensional pattern point can easily be determined geometrically by checking to see on which side of a plane the pattern point resides. As a specific example consider the set of eight patterns shown in Fig. 6·6a. For convenience these patterns are the vertices of a three-dimensional cube. They are numbered as shown for purposes of identification. The planes shown in Fig. 6·6a are the surfaces implemented by three TLUs. The arrows attached to each of the planes point toward the side yielding a $+1$ TLU response.

Suppose that these three TLUs comprise the first layer of a layered machine. The three-dimensional $\mathcal{I}_1$ space is then a cube, centered about the origin, whose vertices represent the eight possible *combinations* of responses of three TLUs. This cube is shown in Fig. 6·6b. If we number the coordinate axes of the image-space cube in accordance with the TLU

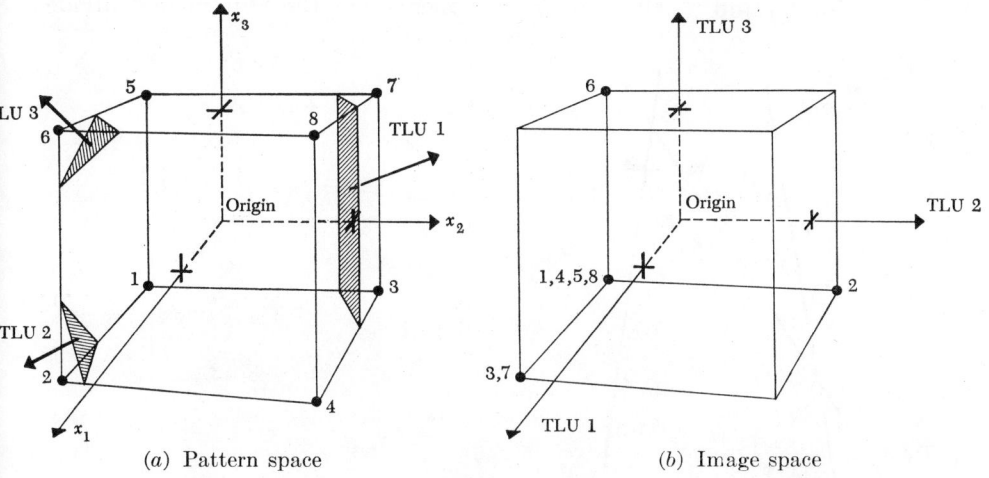

(a) Pattern space (b) Image space

FIGURE 6 · 6 Pattern-space to image-space transformation

numbers 1, 2, and 3, we have an easy means of determining the transformation from the pattern space to the image space. For example, patterns 3 and 7 both yield a response of $+1$ for TLU 1 and a response of -1 for the other TLUs; hence these two patterns are transformed into the single point $(1,-1,-1)$ in image space. The numbers associated with the image points in Fig. 6·6b refer to the patterns which are transformed into each of these image points.

Note that the planes in Fig. 6·6a divide the pattern space into compartments or *cells*. In this example there are four cells that contain pattern points. Two of these cells contain one pattern each; one cell contains four patterns; and one cell contains two patterns. Each nonempty cell in pattern space corresponds to a vertex in $\mathcal{I}_1$ space. Thus, the four patterns 1, 4, 5, and 8 all map into the same image vertex because they all belong to the same cell. In general, there are as many distinct vertices in $\mathcal{I}_1$ space as there are nonempty cells in pattern space.

Let us consider another example in which the patterns are repre-

106   LAYERED MACHINES

sented as points in a two-dimensional space. Suppose these patterns belong to two distinct subsets $\mathfrak{X}_1$ and $\mathfrak{X}_2$ and that we desire to synthesize a two-layer machine to separate these subsets. The pattern points for this example are shown in Fig. 6·7a. In this figure the points marked □ represent patterns belonging to $\mathfrak{X}_1$, and the points marked ○ represent patterns belonging to $\mathfrak{X}_2$.

Clearly the TLUs in the first layer of the desired layered machine must at least implement hyperplanes (lines in two dimensions) which partition $\mathfrak{X}_1$ and $\mathfrak{X}_2$. By *partition* we mean that the hyperplanes divide

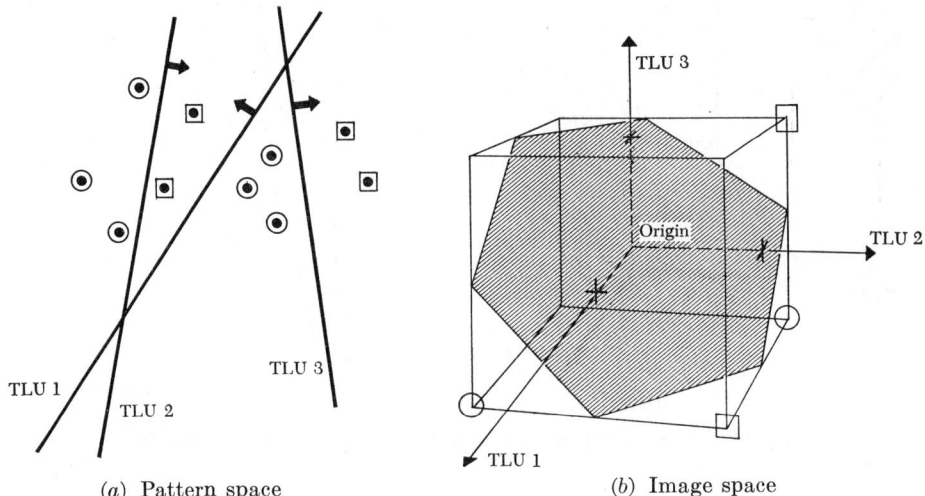

(a) Pattern space   (b) Image space

FIGURE 6·7   Transformations in a two-layer machine

the pattern space into cells such that no two patterns of opposite categorization reside in the same cell. The necessity for partitioning the sets $\mathfrak{X}_1$ and $\mathfrak{X}_2$ arises because corresponding to each nonempty cell in the pattern space is a vertex in $\mathcal{I}_1$ space and this vertex must be associated with only one of the two categories. Figure 6·7a shows three lines which partition $\mathfrak{X}_1$ and $\mathfrak{X}_2$. The arrows denote the positive sides of each line.

The resulting image space is shown in Fig. 6·7b. The symbols □ and ○ are again used to denote the category associated with each image-point vertex. Note that in this example the two subsets $\mathcal{I}_1^{(1)}$ and $\mathcal{I}_2^{(1)}$ of image-space vertices are linearly separable; the plane shown is one which separates these subsets. Thus a two-layer machine with three TLUs in the first layer is adequate for dichotomizing the given pattern subsets.

The plane shown in Fig. 6·7b is normal to the major diagonal of the cube running from the $(-1,-1,-1)$ vertex through the origin to the $(+1,+1,+1)$ vertex. Thus, the plane is normal to the vector $(1,1,1)$, and the TLU in the second layer which implements this plane gives equal weight to each of the three outputs from the first-layer TLUs. That is, this particular two-layer machine is a committee machine. Committee machines always have a fixed hyperplane in the I_1 space, and this hyperplane is the perpendicular bisector of a major diagonal of the image-space cube. The process of training the committee machine is then a search for a pattern-space to image-space transformation such that $\mathcal{G}_1^{(1)}$ and $\mathcal{G}_2^{(2)}$ are placed on opposite sides of the fixed image-space hyperplane.

If the image-space hyperplane is not fixed, then we need only find a transformation which leaves $\mathcal{G}_1^{(1)}$ and $\mathcal{G}_2^{(1)}$ linearly separable. For any given training subsets $\mathfrak{X}_1$ and $\mathfrak{X}_2$ it would be of interest to know necessary and sufficient conditions on the hyperplanes implemented by the first-layer TLUs such that $\mathcal{G}_1^{(1)}$ and $\mathcal{G}_2^{(1)}$ are linearly separable. We know for example that it is necessary that these hyperplanes partition $\mathfrak{X}_1$ and $\mathfrak{X}_2$. A set of conditions that are both necessary and sufficient have not yet been found, but in the next section we shall state some sufficient conditions. When these conditions are met, $\mathcal{G}_1^{(1)}$ and $\mathcal{G}_2^{(1)}$ are guaranteed to be linearly separable, and thus a two-layer machine suffices to perform the pattern dichotomization.

6·6 A sufficient condition for image-space linear separability

Before stating and proving the sufficient condition it will be helpful to make a definition. We have already defined a *partition* of the subsets $\mathfrak{X}_1$ and $\mathfrak{X}_2$. We now define a *nonredundant* partition of $\mathfrak{X}_1$ and $\mathfrak{X}_2$ as a

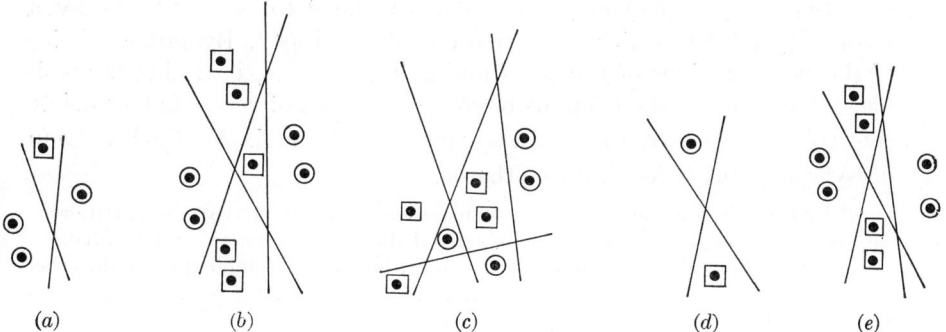

(a) (b) (c) (d) (e)

FIGURE 6·8 Nonredundant (a,b,c,) and redundant (d,e) partitions

108 LAYERED MACHINES

partition with the property that if any one of the separating hyperplanes is removed, at least two nonempty cells will merge into one cell. Some examples of nonredundant and redundant partitions are shown in Fig. 6·8. Note that the partition shown in Fig. 6·7a is also nonredundant. A nonredundant partition is not necessarily one that uses a minimum number of hyperplanes, however. Thus in Fig. 6·8a, one hyperplane (line) would suffice to partition the pattern subsets even though the two hyperplanes shown constitute a nonredundant partition.

We can now state the following theorem.

Theorem 6·1

We are given P hyperplanes* which form a nonredundant partition of two finite subsets $\mathfrak{X}_1$ and $\mathfrak{X}_2$ of pattern vectors. A sufficient condition that $\mathcal{J}_1^{(1)}$ and $\mathcal{J}_2^{(1)}$ be linearly separable is that *exactly $P + 1$ cells formed by the partition be occupied by patterns.*

Proof

We have P TLUs, each of which implements a hyperplane in the pattern space. In this proof it will be convenient for the TLUs to have 0, 1 responses rather than $-1, 1$ responses. Since exactly $P + 1$ cells are occupied by patterns, there are exactly $P + 1$ distinct image-space vertices. Let us form a $P \times (P + 1)$ matrix **M** whose columns are the image-space vertices; **M** is a binary matrix with elements equal to 0 and 1.

Because the partition is nonredundant, if we remove any row from **M**, at least two columns of the reduced matrix will be identical. (Removing a row corresponds to removing a TLU and thus collapsing two cells into one.) A matrix with this property has maximum rank†, thus, rank **M** $= P$.

We shall now show that it is possible to find a weight vector‡ $\mathbf{w} = (w_1, w_2, \ldots, w_P)$ and a threshold value θ to be employed by a second-layer TLU which will separate $\mathcal{J}_1^{(1)}$ and $\mathcal{J}_2^{(1)}$. By proper choice of the positive sides of the partitioning hyperplanes, it is always possible to have one of the columns of **M** be a column of zeros. Let us delete this column from **M** to form a square $P \times P$ matrix $\hat{\mathbf{M}}$. Each column of $\hat{\mathbf{M}}$ is a vertex belonging to either $\mathcal{J}_1^{(1)}$ or $\mathcal{J}_2^{(1)}$.

---

* In the following proof we do not make use of the fact that the partitioning surfaces are hyperplanes. Thus, a more general theorem could actually be stated.

† If rank **M** $< P$, at least one row of **M** must be a linear combination of the other rows. But then the removal of this row from **M** could not result in two columns' becoming identical.

‡ We use the lower-case symbol **w** to denote a P-dimensional weight vector, i.e., one which does not include a $(P + 1)$st component. The role of the $(P + 1)$st component is in this case subsumed by the threshold value θ.

The threshold θ is chosen to be any convenient negative number if the image-space zero vector is a vertex belonging to $\mathcal{J}_1^{(1)}$; otherwise θ is chosen to be any convenient positive number. In this way all the pattern vectors which map into the image-space zero vector are automatically classified correctly.

Clearly, the weight vector **w** has only to satisfy

$$\mathbf{w}\hat{\mathbf{M}} = \mathbf{C} \tag{6.9}$$

where **C** is a row vector whose P components $c_1, c_2, \ldots, c_P$ can be chosen arbitrarily to satisfy

$$\begin{aligned} c_i > \theta & \quad \text{if the } i\text{th column of } \hat{\mathbf{M}} \text{ is a vertex belonging to } \mathcal{J}_1^{(1)} \\ c_i < \theta & \quad \text{if the } i\text{th column of } \hat{\mathbf{M}} \text{ is a vertex belonging to } \mathcal{J}_2^{(1)} \end{aligned} \tag{6.10}$$

Since $\hat{\mathbf{M}}$ has an inverse (it has rank equal to P), we can always solve for **w** by

$$\mathbf{w} = \mathbf{C}\hat{\mathbf{M}}^{-1} \tag{6.11}$$

Thus, since a threshold and weight vector can always be found, the theorem is proved. Note that there is a great amount of freedom allowed in finding a solution vector **w**. After the threshold value θ is chosen, the quantities c_i can be chosen arbitrarily within the constraints given by Eq. (6.10).

One important application of the above theorem can be made if the partitioning hyperplanes implemented by the first-layer TLUs are all parallel. In this case there are exactly $P + 1$ nonempty cells when P planes are used in a nonredundant partition. Hence the resulting image-space vertices are linearly separable. Since two distinct finite subsets of pattern vectors can always be nonredundantly partitioned by a set of parallel hyperplanes, a corollary of the above theorem states that it is *always* possible to find some two-layer machine to dichotomize two distinct, finite subsets. Because of this fact the advantages, if any, of multi-layer pattern dichotomizers over two-layer machines might rest solely on the possibility for a smaller number of first-layer TLUs.

6·7 Derivation of a discriminant function for a layered machine

It was mentioned in Sec. 6·1 that the discriminant functions of layered machines are piecewise linear. In this section, we shall verify this statement.

110   LAYERED MACHINES

Consider the first layer of a layered machine for $R = 2$. Suppose the first layer has P TLUs. Let the binary output of the ith TLU in the first layer be denoted by u_i, and let the weight vector corresponding to this TLU be denoted by $\mathbf{W}_i$. For any given augmented input pattern $\mathbf{Y}$ each $u_i = +1$ or -1, depending on whether $\mathbf{Y} \cdot \mathbf{W}_i$ is greater than or less than zero. Let us denote the dot products $\mathbf{Y} \cdot \mathbf{W}_1, \mathbf{Y} \cdot \mathbf{W}_2, \ldots, \mathbf{Y} \cdot \mathbf{W}_P$ by the symbols $f_1(\mathbf{Y}), f_2(\mathbf{Y}), \ldots, f_P(\mathbf{Y})$, respectively.

Now, still considering the first layer of TLUs, let us look ahead through the remaining layers toward the final response of the layered machine. This response is a two-valued function of the binary numbers

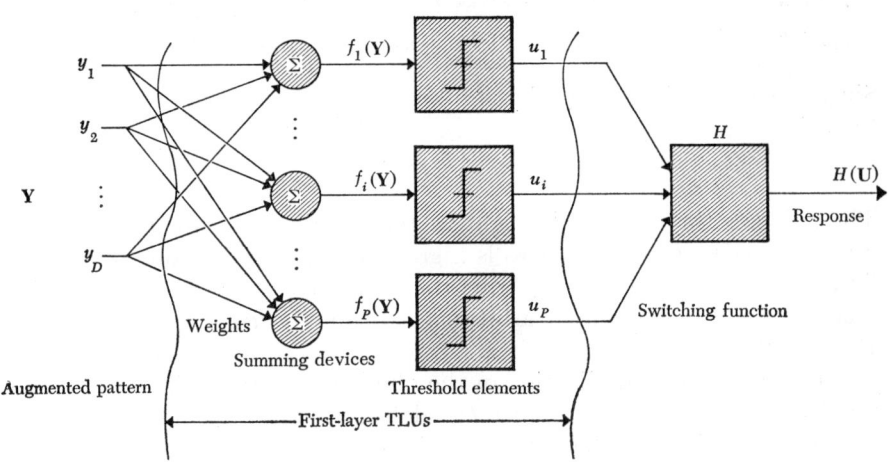

FIGURE 6·9   A general form for layered machines

$u_1, u_2, \ldots, u_P$. Let us define the vector $\mathbf{U} = (u_1, u_2, \ldots, u_P)$. Let $H(\mathbf{U})$ be a two-valued function of the vector $\mathbf{U}$. Such a function is called a *switching function*. If the TLU in the final layer has a response of $+1$ when the outputs of the first layer of TLUs are given by the components of $\mathbf{U}$, then $H(\mathbf{U}) = +1$. If the final TLU has a response of -1, then $H(\mathbf{U}) = -1$.

We thus see that the layers following the first layer could be replaced by any structure implementing the appropriate switching function $H(\mathbf{U})$. Thus, a general form for layered machines is as shown in Fig. 6·9. Note that if P is odd and if $H(\mathbf{U})$ is the majority function (i.e., $H(\mathbf{U}) = +1$ if the majority of the $u_i = +1$), then the layered machine is a committee machine. The effect of training any of the TLUs in the first layer of a layered machine (i.e., to alter their weight vectors) is to adjust the functions $f_1, \ldots, f_P$. The effect of training any of the TLUs in the subsequent layers is to adjust the switching function $H(\mathbf{U})$.

To find the discriminant function of a layered machine, given a set of P functions $f_i(\mathbf{Y})$, $i = 1, \ldots, P$ and a switching function $H(\mathbf{U})$, we must find a $g(\mathbf{X})$ such that

$$
\begin{aligned}
g(\mathbf{X}) &> 0 \quad \text{when } \mathbf{X} \text{ produces a } \mathbf{U} \text{ for which } H(\mathbf{U}) = +1 \\
g(\mathbf{X}) &< 0 \quad \text{when } \mathbf{X} \text{ produces a } \mathbf{U} \text{ for which } H(\mathbf{U}) = -1
\end{aligned} \quad (6\cdot 12)
$$

The discriminant function $g(\mathbf{X})$ can be derived as follows: Suppose that we are given a switching function $H(\mathbf{U})$. Since $\mathbf{U}$ is a binary vector with P components there are 2^P distinct $\mathbf{U}$ vectors. For some of these $\mathbf{U}$ vectors, $H(\mathbf{U}) = 1$, and for the remaining, $H(\mathbf{U}) = -1$. Let $\mathbf{H}_1$ be a matrix whose rows consist of those $\mathbf{U}$ vectors for which $H(\mathbf{U}) = +1$. Let $\mathbf{H}_2$ be a matrix whose rows consist of the remaining $\mathbf{U}$ vectors. If there are L $\mathbf{U}$ vectors for which $H(\mathbf{U}) = +1$, then $\mathbf{H}_1$ will be an $L \times P$ matrix and $\mathbf{H}_2$ will be a $(2^P - L) \times P$ matrix. Both $\mathbf{H}_1$ and $\mathbf{H}_2$ are binary matrices whose elements are equal to $+1$ or -1.

We now define the following vector-valued function:

$$\mathbf{F}(\mathbf{Y}) = \begin{pmatrix} f_1(\mathbf{Y}) \\ f_2(\mathbf{Y}) \\ \ldots \\ f_P(\mathbf{Y}) \end{pmatrix}$$

Consider the column vectors $\mathbf{G}_1(\mathbf{X})$ and $\mathbf{G}_2(\mathbf{X})$ defined in terms of $\mathbf{Y}$ by the expressions

$$
\begin{aligned}
\mathbf{G}_1(\mathbf{X}) &= \mathbf{H}_1 \mathbf{F}(\mathbf{Y}) \\
\mathbf{G}_2(\mathbf{X}) &= \mathbf{H}_2 \mathbf{F}(\mathbf{Y})
\end{aligned} \quad (6\cdot 13)
$$

where $\mathbf{G}_1(\mathbf{X})$ is a vector with L components, and $\mathbf{G}_2(\mathbf{X})$ is a vector with $2^P - L$ components. Let the ith component of $\mathbf{G}_1(\mathbf{X})$ be denoted by $g_1^{(i)}(\mathbf{X})$, $i = 1, \ldots, L$, and let the ith component of $\mathbf{G}_2(\mathbf{X})$ be denoted by $g_2^{(i)}(\mathbf{X})$, $i = 1, \ldots, 2^P - L$. Each $g_1^{(i)}(\mathbf{X})$ and $g_2^{(i)}(\mathbf{X})$ is a linear combination of the $f_j(\mathbf{Y})$, $j = 1, \ldots, P$. Furthermore, in each of these linear combinations, the coefficients of the f_j are equal to plus or minus one. Clearly, for any given vector $\mathbf{X}$ that linear combination whose binary coefficients agree in sign, term for term, with the signs of the f_j for $j = 1, \ldots, P$ will be the largest. Therefore, for any pattern $\mathbf{X}$ producing a $\mathbf{U}$ for which $H(\mathbf{U}) = +1$

$$\max_{i=1,\ldots,L} \{g_1^{(i)}(\mathbf{X})\} > \max_{i=1,\ldots,2^P-L} \{g_2^{(i)}(\mathbf{X})\} \quad (6\cdot 14)$$

and for any pattern $\mathbf{X}$ producing a $\mathbf{U}$ for which $H(\mathbf{U}) = -1$

$$\max_{i=1,\ldots,L} \{g_1^{(i)}(\mathbf{X})\} < \max_{i=1,\ldots,2^P-L} \{g_2^{(i)}(\mathbf{X})\} \qquad (6\cdot 15)$$

Inequalities (6·14) and (6·15) lead us to define the discriminant functions

$$g_1(\mathbf{X}) = \max_{i=1,\ldots,L} \{g_1^{(i)}(\mathbf{X})\}$$

and $\qquad (6\cdot 16)$

$$g_2(\mathbf{X}) = \max_{i=1,\ldots,2^P-L} \{g_2^{(i)}(\mathbf{X})\}$$

Thus, $g(\mathbf{X}) = g_1(\mathbf{X}) - g_2(\mathbf{X})$ can be given by

$$g(\mathbf{X}) = \max_{i=1,\ldots,L} \{g_1^{(i)}(\mathbf{X})\} - \max_{i=1,\ldots,2^P-L} \{g_2^{(i)}(\mathbf{X})\} \qquad (6\cdot 17)$$

or

$$g(\mathbf{X}) = \max_{i=1,\ldots,L} \{g_1^{(i)}(\mathbf{X})\} + \min_{i=1,\ldots,2^P-L} \{-g_2^{(i)}(\mathbf{X})\} \qquad (6\cdot 18)$$

The individual discriminant functions defined by Eq. (6·16) are comprised of pieces of a number of "subsidiary" discriminant functions. These subsidiary functions are the $g_1^{(i)}(\mathbf{X})$ and the $g_2^{(i)}(\mathbf{X})$. Examination of Eq. (6·13) reveals that each subsidiary discriminant function is a linear combination of the functions $f_1, \ldots, f_P$. Since each of the $f_1, \ldots, f_P$ is a linear function of the pattern vector, the subsidiary discriminant functions are also linear. Thus, according to the definitions made in Sec. 2·7, a layered machine is a piecewise linear machine.

A layered machine with P TLUs in the first layer has a total of 2^P linear subsidiary discriminant functions; these are divided into two classes (corresponding to category 1 and category 2) depending on the nature of the switching function $H(\mathbf{U})$ implemented by the subsequent layers. It must be pointed out, however, that these 2^P subsidiary discriminant functions are not independent but are linearly related through Eq. (6·13). Since there are only P TLUs in the first layer there can be at most only P linearly independent subsidiary discriminant functions. A layered machine is therefore a piecewise linear machine whose 2^P subsidiary discriminant functions are constrained by the Eq. (6·13).

The constraints just mentioned may act to make questions regarding the properties and training methods of layered machines less tractable than might be the corresponding questions for unconstrained piecewise linear machines. With this thought in mind, in the next chapter we shall turn our attention to general piecewise linear machines.

6·8 Bibliographical and historical remarks

Pattern-classifying TLU networks have been studied by Farley and Clark,[1] Rosenblatt,[2] Widrow,[3] Brain et al.,[4] and others. The simple α perceptron proposed by Rosenblatt is a two-layer machine consisting of a first layer of fixed TLUs followed by a single trainable TLU in the second layer. (Rosenblatt speaks of the α perceptron as a three-layer structure because he thinks of the pattern inputs as being generated by a first layer of "sensory units.")

The training rule described in Sec. 6·3 for the committee machine was first proposed by Ridgway.[5] Note that the committee machine and the α perceptron have a similar structure; they are both two-layer machines. Each has one layer of trainable TLUs; they differ only in which layer is trained. Machines of this type have been studied by Widrow[3] (who calls them MADALINES for *multiple* ADALINES) and by Kaylor.[6] Efron[7] proved that the fixed-increment error-correction training method implied a bound on the length of the weight vectors, thus explaining some cases in which the committee machine cannot be successfully trained.

REFERENCES

1 Farley, B., and W. Clark: Simulation of Self-organizing Systems by Digital Computer, *Trans. IRE on Info. Theory, PGIT*-4, pp. 76–84, September, 1954.
2 Rosenblatt, F.: "Principles of Neurodynamics: Perceptrons and the Theory of Brain Mechanisms," Spartan Books, Washington, D.C., 1961.
3 Widrow, B.: Generalization and Information Storage in Networks of Adaline 'Neurons,' in Yovits, Jacobi, and Goldstein (eds.), "Self-organizing Systems —1962," pp. 435–461, Spartan Books, Washington, D.C., 1962.
4 Brain, A. E., et al.: A Large, Self-contained Learning Machine, 1963 *WESCON Paper* 6.1, August, 1963.
5 Ridgway, W. C.: An Adaptive Logic System with Generalizing Properties, *Stanford Electronics Laboratories Technical Report* 1556-1, prepared under Air

Force Contract AF 33(616)-7726, Stanford University, Stanford, California, April, 1962.
6 Kaylor, D. J.: A Mathematical Model of a Two-layer Network of Threshold Elements, *Rome Air Development Center Technical Documentary Report RADC-TDR*-63-534, March, 1964.
7 Efron, B.: The Perceptron Correction Procedure in Nonseparable Situations, *Rome Air Development Center Technical Documentary Report RADC-TDR*-63-533, February, 1964.

CHAPTER 7

PIECEWISE LINEAR MACHINES

7·1 Multimodal pattern-classifying tasks

Piecewise linear (PWL) machines were originally defined in Chapter 2. The general form for such machines was illustrated in Fig. 2·6. A PWL machine consists of R discriminators, where R is the number of pattern categories. Each discriminator employs a number of subsidiary linear discriminant functions. Thus a PWL machine consists of R banks of subsidiary discriminators, each bank corresponding to one of the pattern categories.

The machine classifies patterns as follows: A pattern $\mathbf{X}$ is presented to the machine and the values of all of the subsidiary linear discriminants are measured. The pattern is then placed in the category corresponding to the bank containing the highest-valued subsidiary discriminant.

We have seen (Chapter 2) that PWL machines can perform minimum-distance classifications with respect to finite point sets. For an example, refer to Fig. 2·7; it can be seen that a PWL machine can determine whether a given pattern is closer to the point set $\mathcal{P}_1$ than it is to the point set $\mathcal{P}_2$ and can accordingly place the pattern in category 1 or category 2. Such a classification rule is useful if for each category there is more than one "prototype" or typical pattern around which all other patterns in the category cluster. We shall say in this case that there is more than one *mode* per category. Suppose that there are L_i prototype patterns for the ith category and that all patterns belonging to category i are close to one of these prototypes. Then, a PWL machine with L_i linear discriminators in the L_ith bank might be an appropriate pattern classifier.

Pattern-classifying tasks that have many different prototype patterns per category are common. The weather-prediction example of Chapter 1 can be used to illustrate such a multimodal task. Suppose that a pattern-classifying machine is to be used to classify weather measurements into two categories: Those which precede fog at a certain coastal airport and those which do not. The presence of fog may be caused by any of several quite different weather situations. Fog may be produced by the confluence of warm, moist sea air and cold, continental air or it may result from the chilling of moist surface air by a cold air mass above the surface. Each of these different weather situations could be typified by a different prototype pattern of weather measurements; yet, the patterns surrounding each of these prototypes all belong to the *single* category of fog.

Because so many pattern-classifying tasks are of this multimodal type, PWL machines are an important and useful class. In this chapter we shall discuss some of the problems connected with training PWL machines. Unfortunately, not very much is yet known about the properties of PWL machines. Since the piecewise linear discriminant functions are not Φ functions, the error-correction training theorems proved in Chapter 5 do not apply to PWL machines. The pattern capacity of PWL machines is also unknown. Even though well-developed theory is lacking, some speculations have been advanced that we shall discuss.

7·2 Training PWL machines

The problem of training a PWL machine has two aspects. First, the subsidiary linear discriminant functions must be adjusted in some appropriate manner. Such adjustments are effected by changing the weight vector associated with each of the subsidiary discriminators. If the PWL machine has a total of L subsidiary discriminators, there will be a total of L weight vectors to be adjusted. Second, the subsidiary discriminators must be organized into R banks. This organization should be regarded as a training problem since it might be unknown beforehand how many subsidiary discriminators should be in each bank. Thus, training also involves shuffling the subsidiary discriminators from bank to bank until some appropriate organization is found.*

What is needed, then, to train PWL machines is a method of adjusting weight vectors and a method for transferring them from bank to bank. Preferably, these training procedures should be iterative so that complicated analyses of large pattern sets might be avoided. The simplest, and perhaps most desirable, procedure would involve forming a training sequence of patterns and presenting these patterns, one at a time, to the machine. At each pattern presentation the machine may be adjusted by changing weight vectors, by transferring weight vectors among the banks, or both.

The second aspect of training might be avoided by ensuring a surplus of subsidiary discriminators in each bank, although such an exuberant use of subsidiary discriminators might be grossly uneconomical. If the total number of subsidiary discriminators were limited, it might then become necessary to be able to move subsidiary discriminators from banks where they were not needed to banks where they were needed.

No satisfactory iterative methods have yet been proposed for transferring weight vectors among the banks,† although we shall present in this chapter some training methods for adjusting the subsidiary discriminant functions. We shall conclude this section by proposing an intuitively appealing error-correction training procedure for PWL machines. (Recall that an error-correction procedure is one for which adjustments are made only if the machine responds incorrectly to a pattern.) The following procedure is suggested as a training method for adjusting the subsidiary

---

* In the case of layered machines with $R = 2$ and P TLUs in the first layer, these dual aspects of training have the following significances. There are 2^P subsidiary discriminant functions; their adjustment is accomplished by adjusting the linear functions $f_1, f_2, \ldots, f_P$. Such adjustments are made by modifying the weight values of the first layer of TLUs. The shuffling of the subsidiary discriminators between the two banks corresponds to changing the switching function $H(\mathbf{U})$. Such changes are accomplished by changing the weight values of the subsequent layers of TLUs. Thus the two aspects of training general PWL machines are intimately related with the problem of simultaneous training of multiple layers in a layered machine.

† Perhaps it would be useful to regard the matter of transferring weight vectors among the banks in terms of a birth and death process and a pool of "extra" weight vectors. Whenever a weight vector is found to be superfluous within a given bank, it should be transferred from that bank to the pool (death). Whenever a bank needs an extra weight vector, one should be transferred to that bank from the pool—provided that the pool is not empty (birth). What is needed now are rules defining when a weight vector within a bank is no longer needed there and when a new weight vector is needed within a bank.

118 PIECEWISE LINEAR MACHINES

discriminant functions while leaving their distributions within the banks fixed. Training patterns are presented to the PWL machine whose R banks of subsidiary linear discriminant functions have initially been selected arbitrarily. After presenting a pattern which the machine classifies correctly, we make no changes in the values of the weights used to implement the subsidiary discriminant functions. Suppose, however, that a pattern $\mathbf{Y}_k$ belonging to category i causes an incorrect response. Such would be the case if the jth bank, $j \neq i$, contained the largest subsidiary discriminant. The adjustment method first subtracts $\mathbf{Y}_k$ from the weight vector used by this subsidiary discriminant function in the jth bank. Of those subsidiary discriminant functions in the ith bank, we next determine which has the *largest* value for $\mathbf{Y}_k$. The corresponding weight vector is adjusted by the addition of $\mathbf{Y}_k$. The intuitive basis for such a procedure is clear; it is an attempt to apply something like the generalized error-correction procedure to a structure containing more than one subsidiary discriminant function per bank. The conditions (if any) under which this procedure terminates in a solution, when a solution exists, have not yet been determined.

7 · 3   A disadvantage of the error-correction training methods

Throughout this book we have discussed several nonparametric training methods. Generally, nonparametric training methods are to be preferred to parametric ones because no assumptions need be made about the forms of underlying probability distributions. This advantage is especially important in multimodal pattern-classifying tasks.

The nonparametric rules that we have discussed so far have all been error-correction rules, and it must be said that such rules do suffer from an important disadvantage. This disadvantage results from the fact that error-correction rules never allow an error in pattern classification without making some adjustment in the discriminant functions. In many pattern-classification tasks, it may be necessary to tolerate some small number of classification errors in the training set in order to classify related patterns with a small probability of error. This is so because the underlying probability distributions may be sufficiently overlapping that the optimum decision surfaces do not perfectly separate the training subsets.

Consider, for example, the following dichotomization problem: It is known that there are two categories of patterns, and we have two training subsets that are representative of these two categories. We may assume that there do exist probability distributions for each category, although we are unwilling to make any assumption about the forms of these distributions. (Suppose, however, that in reality these distributions are given by normal probability-density functions which overlap to some significant extent.) If the covariance matrices of the normal densities are equal, then the decision surface which minimizes the probability of error is a hyperplane perpendicular to the line segment joining the means of the two density functions. It should be observed that if the two density functions overlap sufficiently, it is likely that this optimum decision surface will not perfectly separate all the members of the two training subsets.

If we were willing to assume initially that these distributions were normal, then the parametric training methods outlined in Chapter 3 would lead to a decision surface closely approximating the optimum surface if the training subsets were large enough. However, we are now pretending that such an assumption was initially unwarranted, and therefore we are limiting ourselves to nonparametric training methods. Suppose that we decided to use an error-correction training procedure to train a single TLU. Even though a TLU is capable of implementing the optimum decision surface, an error-correction procedure could never stabilize at the optimum surface since inevitable errors would cause an adjustment away from this surface. Furthermore, the situation is not helped by using error-correction procedures to adjust more complex decision surfaces (such as Φ surfaces or piecewise linear surfaces) even though it may be possible to achieve a perfect separation of the *training* subsets with these more complex surfaces. The reason that performance is not improved is that in this case the complex surfaces are not optimum. Even though they may separate the training subsets perfectly, they will lead to higher error probabilities in classifying related patterns.

Experience with error-correction procedures is insufficient to permit evaluating the seriousness of this disadvantage. In any case, certain modifications of the error-correction procedures and other nonparametric procedures are being studied for application to "overlapping" pattern subsets. In the next few sections we shall develop some nonparametric procedures for training PWL machines that do not depend on the error-correction principle.

7·4 A nonparametric decision procedure

Several nonparametric decision methods exist which do not use the error-correction principle. Most of these place much emphasis on the distances between a pattern to be classified and members of the training subsets. Sometimes the distance used is not simple Euclidean distance, but some function that depends on the geometric arrangement of the patterns in the training subsets. Many of these nonparametric rules actually lead to the same discriminant functions that would be obtained by parametric training and the assumptions that the pattern probability distributions are normal.[3]

There does exist a simple nonparametric rule, however, whose use implies only that the probability-density functions exist and that they are continuous. We shall call this rule the *Fix and Hodges* method.[2]

To determine the discriminant functions by the Fix and Hodges method, we first select some large positive integer k, which is small compared to the number of patterns in each of the training subsets. Next we select some metric with which to measure distance in the pattern space; for example, we might select ordinary Euclidean distance. Now, to classify an arbitrary pattern $\mathbf{X}$, we pool the patterns in the R training subsets $\mathfrak{X}_1$, $\mathfrak{X}_2, \ldots, \mathfrak{X}_R$ and find those k patterns which are closest to $\mathbf{X}$. Suppose that of these k closest patterns n_1 patterns belong to $\mathfrak{X}_1$, n_2 patterns belong to $\mathfrak{X}_2, \ldots,$ and n_R patterns belong to $\mathfrak{X}_R$ $(n_1 + n_2 + \cdots + n_R = k)$. We then set

$$g_1(\mathbf{X}) = n_1$$
$$g_2(\mathbf{X}) = n_2$$
$$\ldots$$
$$g_R(\mathbf{X}) = n_R$$

(7·1)

and make a decision regarding the category of $\mathbf{X}$ by selecting the largest discriminant as usual.

The Fix and Hodges procedure clearly is an attempt to estimate the values of $p(\mathbf{X}|i)\, p(i)$ for $i = 1, \ldots, R$ around the point $\mathbf{X}$. If these values are approximated by the numbers $n_1, n_2, \ldots, n_R$, then the specification of the $g_i(\mathbf{X})$ by Eq. (7·1) follows directly from Eq. (3·7a). Note, therefore, that the Fix and Hodges method, as we have described it, assumes a loss function which weights all classification errors equally.

Selection of the integer k is quite important in the application of the Fix and Hodges procedure. If k is too small the $g_i(\mathbf{X})$ will vary rapidly with $\mathbf{X}$, and the consequent decision surfaces will be highly sensitive to the spatial locations of the training patterns. If k is too large (in relation to the number of patterns in the training subsets) the $g_i(\mathbf{X})$ will not be sensitive enough to the actual variations of the probability distributions with $\mathbf{X}$. In any case, if the training subsets are small, the estimates n_1, $n_2, \ldots, n_R$ will not be good ones (neither would any other estimates). If the training subsets are large, it has been shown[2] that the Fix and Hodges decision rule leads to the same decisions as would be made if the (unknown) probability distributions were known and used in Eq. (3·7a). In general, the value of k should increase without limit with increasing N, if N is the total number of patterns in the training subsets. The value of k/N, however, should decrease toward zero with increasing N.

The high storage requirements of the Fix and Hodges method render it impractical in most pattern-classification tasks. To classify any pattern **X**, the distance between **X** and each of the patterns in the training subsets must be computed. If these computations are to be performed rapidly, each of the training patterns must be stored (as weight vectors, for example) in some rapid-access memory. Because the method works best when the number of training patterns is large, the storage requirements are often excessive. This disadvantage motivates a search for other nonparametric methods which preserve some of the features of the Fix and Hodges method without requiring the individual storage of every training pattern in a rapid-access memory. We shall discuss one such method in the next section.

7·5 Nonparametric decisions based on distances to modes

Rather than storing a large number of training patterns, it may prove feasible to store only a few "typical" training patterns. Each typical pattern selected for storage might actually represent many training patterns that cluster around it in the pattern space. Thus each typical pattern for a given category might be thought of as a "mode" of the probability-density function for that category. We use the word *mode* here to denote the location of a local maximum in the probability-density function.

The nonparametric decision rule to be described assumes the existence of a method to find good estimates for these modes, given the training subsets. Suppose the modes for the various categories, as established by a training procedure, are given by the points $\mathbf{P}_i^{(j)}$ for $i = 1, \ldots, R$ and $j = 1, \ldots, L_i$. That is, there are L_1 typical patterns belonging to category 1, L_2 belonging to category 2, etc.

Then, given these modes, one reasonable way to classify some arbitrary pattern **X** is to measure its distance to each of the modes and place it in that category having the nearest mode. But this procedure is just a minimum-distance-classification rule with respect to point sets. The points belonging to the ith point set $\mathcal{P}_i$ are just the L_i modes $\mathbf{P}_i^{(j)}$ for $j = 1, \ldots, L_i$. Such a minimum-distance classification can, of course, be achieved by a PWL machine whose discriminant functions are given by Eq. (2·17).

Since the number of modes is usually much smaller than the number of training patterns, the rapid-access storage requirements for this method are much less demanding than those for the Fix and Hodges method. The concept of distance still plays an important role in a way which preserves some of the features of the Fix and Hodges method. It seems reasonable to assume that the k closest training patterns to a given pattern $\mathbf{X}$ will often include a predominant number of patterns from the cluster surrounding the closest mode. Thus the "closest-mode" method just described will often make decisions identical to those made by the Fix and Hodges method. What is needed to apply the closest-mode method is a means of training a PWL machine such that the modes are identified and the appropriate discriminant functions are set up. This training process should be an iterative one, operating on a sequence of patterns from the training set. In the next section we shall present a candidate training method.

7·6 Mode-seeking and related training methods for PWL machines

To apply the closest-mode decision method, we need a training procedure to locate the modes or centers of high pattern density. Suppose that we have a PWL machine whose subsidiary discriminant functions are represented by the weight vectors* $\mathbf{w}_i^{(j)}$ for $i = 1, \ldots, R$ and $j = 1, \ldots, L_i$. Thus there are R banks of weight vectors, and the ith bank has L_i members. Any training method which adjusts the weight vectors in each bank so that each weight vector finally resides in the center of a cluster of like-category patterns will be called a *mode-seeking* training method. (We assume that the weight vectors in the ith bank are adjusted toward the centers of clusters belonging to category i only for all $i = 1, \ldots, R$.) In addition to locating the weight vectors of a PWL machine in the centers of pattern clusters, the training procedure must adjust the $(d+1)$st weight components such that

$$w^{(j)}{}_{i,d+1} = -\tfrac{1}{2} \mathbf{w}_i^{(j)} \cdot \mathbf{w}_i^{(j)} \quad \text{for } i = 1, \ldots, R, j = 1, \ldots, L_i \quad (7\cdot2)$$

are satisfied.

If Eq. (7·2) is satisfied, and if the training process successfully locates weight vectors at the modes, then the PWL machine so trained will implement a closest-mode decision rule with ordinary Euclidean distance as a criterion. We have now to discuss possible mode-seeking training rules for the weight vectors where we assume that Eq. (7·2) will be used to establish the values for the $(d+1)$st components.

* We use the lower-case symbol $\mathbf{w}$ again to denote a d-dimensional weight vector, i.e., one which does not include the $(d+1)$st component. The $(d+1)$st component will be treated separately; $\mathbf{w}_i^{(j)}$ denotes the jth weight vector in the ith bank.

The problem of estimating modes is generally much more difficult than that of estimating the mean of a distribution. The sample mean or center of gravity of a set of points usually serves as a good estimate for the mean of the probability distribution of which the points are samples. It is true that if the probability distribution has only one mode (unimodal), then the center of gravity of a set of points is often a good estimate for this mode. In multimodal situations, the picture is quite different; here, the center of gravity of a set of points drawn from a multimodal distribution is often useless for pattern classifying.

The following training method is presented because it illustrates several that have been proposed for mode seeking. No rigorous theoretical treatment has been advanced to support it, and only limited empirical evidence has been collected to justify its use, but it does appear intuitively attractive. Suppose that patterns are presented to the PWL machine one at a time from a training sequence. Let the initial weight vectors be selected arbitrarily.* We shall describe the adjustments to be made at the kth step. Suppose that the $(k + 1)$st pattern in the training sequence is $\mathbf{X}_{k+1}$, a member of category i. Which of the weight vectors belonging to the ith bank is the closest to $\mathbf{X}_{k+1}$ can now be determined, using the PWL machine itself if Eq. (7·2) is used to provide continuous adjustments to the $(d + 1)$st components. Suppose that the jth weight vector in this bank is the closest one to $\mathbf{X}_{k+1}$. Then, only this closest weight vector is adjusted and all other weight vectors (including all those in the other banks) are left fixed. The adjustment made to this closest weight vector is to move it part way along a line directed toward the pattern $\mathbf{X}_{k+1}$.

Let us denote the weight vector which is to be adjusted at this step by the symbol $\mathbf{w}_i^{(j)}[k]$. [The superscript (j) and the subscript i denote that this weight vector is the jth member of the ith bank.] The adjusted weight vector $\mathbf{w}_i^{(j)}[k + 1]$ is then expressed by

$$\mathbf{w}_i^{(j)}[k + 1] = \frac{N\mathbf{w}_i^{(j)}[k] + \mathbf{X}_{k+1}}{N + 1} \qquad (7·3)$$

where N is the number of times that this weight vector had been adjusted before. Thus, the change in the weight vector is calculated to treat equally all the patterns affecting it. Other averages could be used; in particular, it may be advantageous to weight recent patterns more strongly than patterns occurring earlier in the training sequence.

The reader is invited to test the above rule graphically using sample clusters of two-dimensional patterns. Each pattern is considered in sequence and the closest weight vector from the bank belong to the same category as the pattern is moved toward that pattern. After many steps,

---

* One possible selection is to set each of them equal to a different training pattern.

the actual motions become smaller and smaller at each step due to the averaging process. Eventually the weight vectors settle down at locations which are centers of gravity of subsets of the patterns.

The above training process for the closest-mode method does involve some calculations whose implementation might present difficulties. First, one must calculate the $(d + 1)$th components given by Eq. (7·2); second, one must form the average implied by Eq. (7·3) whenever a weight vector is to be adjusted. Among the modifications which might be suggested to alleviate these difficulties are the following.

First, let us set the $\mathbf{w}^{(j)}{}_{i,d+1}$ for $i = 1, \ldots, R$ and $j = 1, \ldots, L_i$ forever equal to zero instead of using Eq. (7·2). (This modification is equivalent to assuming that the weight vectors always have equal lengths.) The classification rule itself can be the same as before: A pattern $\mathbf{X}$ is placed in the category corresponding to the bank having the largest discriminant, although the largest discriminant no longer necessarily corresponds to the closest weight vector since Eq. (7·2) has been violated. Next we modify the training rule as follows: Suppose that the $(k + 1)$th element of the training sequence is $\mathbf{X}_{k+1}$, a member of category i. Select the largest discriminant in the ith bank; suppose it to be produced by the jth weight vector in the ith bank. Then, instead of using Eq. (7·3) to modify this weight vector, we use the familiar expression

$$\mathbf{w}_i^{(j)}[k + 1] = \mathbf{w}_i^{(j)}[k] + c\mathbf{X}_{k+1} \tag{7·4}$$

where the correction increment c is a positive constant. All other weight vectors are left unaltered at this step.

This modification avoids the averaging necessary in the mode-seeking training method. Without this averaging, the weight vectors will not travel toward the center of the clusters; at best, they will eventually point in the directions of the modes. Their lengths would then be roughly proportional to the number of patterns in the cluster toward which each is directed. Because the discriminants are dot products between the pattern vector and the weight vectors, there will be a tendency for the longest weight vectors to produce the largest discriminants [a difficulty which observance of Eq. (7·2) would have prevented]. This tendency may not be harmful, however, since it favors those categories having the most heavily populated clusters (a bias ordinarily prescribed through the a priori probabilities).

The reader may think of other training methods for PWL machines. The final test of any of these methods is in their efficiency and performance in actual pattern-classifying tasks. Since this testing has only just begun, a thorough treatment of the subject of PWL machines must be saved for another story.

7·7 Bibliographical and historical remarks

Some of the material presented in this chapter originated with the author, although his opinions were influenced by many. We shall try to give a short account of these influences here. The disadvantage of the error-correction methods, discussed in Sec. 7·3, has been recognized by several workers. Duda and Singleton[1] have studied and experimented with nonparametric training rules that appear to escape this disadvantage.

The Fix and Hodges method, presented in Sec. 7·4, is the obvious R-category generalization of the two-category method whose properties were studied by Fix and Hodges.[2] Achieving a reduction in storage requirements by ignoring all patterns except the modes was suggested by Sebestyen.[3,4]

Closest-mode classification methods and mode-seeking training have been discussed by many workers. Sebestyen[3,4] proposed a process that he called "Adaptive Sample Set Construction" to find typical patterns or modes. Firschein and Fischler[5] speak of the different modes within a single category as *subclasses* and propose a method to identify them. Jakowatz, Shuey, and White[6] discuss a related problem in waveform recognition in which there are two subclasses (signal plus noise and noise alone) to be identified. It is assumed in their work that the training set cannot be divided into two subsets corresponding to signal and no signal; therefore, it is as if there were only one category of patterns ($R = 1$) but two subclasses within this category that must be learned without benefit of a teacher. (Such situations are often described by the phrase "learning without a teacher.")

The mode-seeking training rule described in Sec. 7·6 was originally proposed and tested by Stark, Okajima, and Whipple.[7] They applied the rule in a simulated PWL machine for the recognition of electrocardiograph signals. It is known that there are several different "typical" electrocardiograph signals representing various types of normal and abnormal heart conditions. The results of their experiments show the efficiency of using mode-seeking training procedures for a PWL categorizer.

The author has also benefited from several discussions with G. Ball and D. Hall of the Stanford Research Institute concerning their mode-seeking training procedure called ISODATA.[8] The ISODATA process also moves weight vectors toward the centers of clusters by a series of iterative adjustments. Each adjustment is influenced by the whole subset of training patterns, however, rather than by a single pattern in turn as in some of the other mode-seeking techniques. Ball and Hall also have provisions for the birth and death of weight vectors during the adjustment procedure.

REFERENCES

1 Duda, R. O., and R. C. Singleton: Training a Threshold Logic Unit with Imperfectly Classified Patterns, paper presented at 1964 WESCON, August 26–29, 1964.
2 Fix, E., and J. L. Hodges, Jr.: Discriminatory Analysis, Nonparametric Discrimination: Consistency Properties, *Project* 21-49-004, *Report* 4, prepared at the University of California under Contract AF 41(128)-31, USAF School of Aviation Medicine, Randolph Field, Texas, February, 1951. (This report may be obtained through the Defense Documentation Center for Scientific and Technical Information, Cameron Station, Alexandria, Virginia. Refer to ATI 110633.)
3 Sebestyen, G.: "Decision-making Processes in Pattern Recognition," The Macmillan Company, New York, 1962.
4 ———: Pattern Recognition by an Adaptive Process of Sample Set Construction, *Trans. IRE on Info. Theory*, vol. 178, no. 5, pp. S82–S91, September, 1962.
5 Firschein, O., and M. Fischler: Automatic Subclass Determination for Pattern-recognition Applications, *Trans. IEEE on Elect. Computers*, vol. EC-12, no. 2, pp. 137–141, April, 1963.
6 Jakowatz, C. V., R. L. Shuey, and G. M. White: Adaptive Waveform Recognition, in C. Cherry (ed.), *Proc. Fourth London Symposium on Information Theory*, Butterworth, Ltd., London, England, 1961.
7 Stark, L., M. Okajima, and G. H. Whipple: Computer Pattern Recognition Techniques: Electrocardiographic Diagnosis, *Comm. of the ACM*, vol. 5, pp. 527–532, October, 1962.
8 Ball, G. H., and D. J. Hall: Some Fundamental Concepts and Synthesis Procedures for Pattern Recognition Preprocessors, paper presented at the International Conference on Microwaves, Circuit Theory, and Information Theory, September 7–11, 1964, Tokyo, Japan.

APPENDIX

AN ALTERNATIVE IMPLEMENTATION OF QUADRIC DISCRIMINANT FUNCTIONS

A·1 Separation of a quadratic form into positive and negative parts

Consider the quadric function

$$g(\mathbf{X}) = \mathbf{X}^t \mathbf{A} \mathbf{X} + \mathbf{B}^t \mathbf{X} + C \qquad (\text{A·1})$$

where $\mathbf{A}$ is a real, $d \times d$, symmetric matrix, $\mathbf{B}$ is a d-dimensional column vector, and C is a scalar. The first term on the right-hand side of Eq. (A·1) is a quadratic form. We shall show that it is always possible to find a pair of real orthogonal matrices $\mathbf{T}_1$ and $\mathbf{T}_2$ and a pair of real diagonal matrices $\mathbf{D}_1$ and $\mathbf{D}_2$ such that the quadratic form can be separated into positive and negative parts as

$$\mathbf{X}^t \mathbf{A} \mathbf{X} = |\mathbf{X}^t \mathbf{D}_1 \mathbf{T}_1|^2 - |\mathbf{X}^t \mathbf{D}_2 \mathbf{T}_2|^2 \qquad (\text{A·2})$$

This altered expression for the quadratic form suggests an interesting method of implementing the quadric function $g(\mathbf{X})$, as we shall soon see.

A well-known result of matrix theory[*] states that for any real, sym-

---

[*] R. Bellman, "Introduction to Matrix Analysis," chap. 4, McGraw-Hill Book Company, New York, 1960.

metric matrix **A** there exists a square real, orthogonal matrix **T** such that

$$\mathbf{T}^t \mathbf{A} \mathbf{T} = \mathbf{\Lambda} \tag{A·3}$$

where $\mathbf{\Lambda}$ is a real, diagonal matrix. Moreover, **T** can always be selected so that the first p_1 diagonal elements of $\mathbf{\Lambda}$ are positive, the next p_2 diagonal elements are negative, and the last $d - (p_1 + p_2)$ diagonal elements are zero, where d is the order of **A**, and $(p_1 + p_2)$ is the rank of **A**. The diagonal elements of $\mathbf{\Lambda}$ are the eigenvalues of **A**, and the columns of **T** are the corresponding unit eigenvectors.

Let us now define the real, diagonal matrices

$$\mathbf{D}_1 = \begin{bmatrix} \lambda_1 & & 0 \\ & \ddots & \\ 0 & & \lambda_{p_1} \end{bmatrix}$$

and

$$\mathbf{D}_2 = \begin{bmatrix} -\lambda_{p_1+1} & & 0 \\ & \ddots & \\ 0 & & -\lambda_{p_1+p_2} \end{bmatrix} \tag{A·4}$$

where $\lambda_1, \ldots, \lambda_{p_1}$ are the first p_1 diagonal elements of $\mathbf{\Lambda}$, and $\lambda_{p_1+1}, \ldots, \lambda_{p_1+p_2}$ are the next p_2 diagonal elements of $\mathbf{\Lambda}$.

Now let $\mathbf{T}_1$ be a $d \times p_1$ matrix consisting of the first p_1 columns of **T**, and let $\mathbf{T}_2$ be a $d \times p_2$ matrix consisting of the next p_2 columns of **T**. Because **T** is orthogonal we can write Eq. (A·3) as follows:

$$\mathbf{A} = \mathbf{T} \mathbf{\Lambda} \mathbf{T}^t \tag{A·5}$$

In terms of the matrices just defined, Eq. (A·5) then becomes

$$\mathbf{A} = \mathbf{T}_1 \mathbf{D}_1 \mathbf{D}_1^t \mathbf{T}_1^t - \mathbf{T}_2 \mathbf{D}_2 \mathbf{D}_2^t \mathbf{T}_2^t \tag{A·6}$$

from which Eq. (A·2) follows immediately.

A·2 Implementation

To simplify our notation we define the following matrices

$$\mathbf{Q}_1 = \mathbf{D}_1^t \mathbf{T}_1^t = [q_{ij}^{(1)}] \tag{A·7}$$

$$\mathbf{Q}_2 = \mathbf{D}_2^t \mathbf{T}_2^t = [q_{ij}^{(2)}] \tag{A·8}$$

AN ALTERNATIVE IMPLEMENTATION

The quadric function $g(\mathbf{X})$ can now be written as

$$g(\mathbf{X}) = |\mathbf{Q}_1\mathbf{X}|^2 - |\mathbf{Q}_2\mathbf{X}|^2 + \mathbf{B}^t\mathbf{X} + C \tag{A·9}$$

Equation (A·9) suggests an implementation employing weights and summers. The term $|\mathbf{Q}_1\mathbf{X}|^2$ is computed by summing the squares of the outputs of p_1 summers, and $|\mathbf{Q}_2\mathbf{X}|^2$ is computed by summing the squares of the outputs of p_2 summers. The implementation shown in Fig. A·1 is a quadric discriminator containing adjustable weights and coefficients that can be set according to Eqs. (A·7) and (A·8). The coefficients following the squarers are set at plus *one* or minus *one*, depending on whether the corresponding summer is computing an element of $\mathbf{Q}_1\mathbf{X}$ or of $\mathbf{Q}_2\mathbf{X}$. [If $p_1 + p_2 < d$, the coefficients of $d - (p_1 + p_2)$ summers can be set equal to zero.]

The implementation of Fig. A·1 is to be compared with that of Fig. 2·8. The former requires roughly twice as many weights but fewer multipliers or squarers than does the latter. Although in Fig. 2·8, the same set of multipliers can be used for each of the R discriminators, each discriminator in Fig. A·1 *must* have its own set of squarers. The exact numbers of these components needed are listed in Table A·1. Unfortunately, the implementation of Fig. A·1 cannot be trained in a straightforward manner by the error-correction training procedures for Φ functions because the weights of Fig. A·1 do not occur linearly as parameters of $g(\mathbf{X})$. The weights of Fig. 2·8 do occur linearly as parameters of $g(\mathbf{X})$, so that training of the structure is readily accomplished.

TABLE A · 1 The numbers of components needed by the two methods of implementing quadric functions

Figure	Number of adjustable weights and coefficients	Number of multipliers and squarers
A·1	$(d+1)^2$	d
2·8	$\dfrac{(d+1)(d+2)}{2}$	$\dfrac{d(d+1)}{2}$

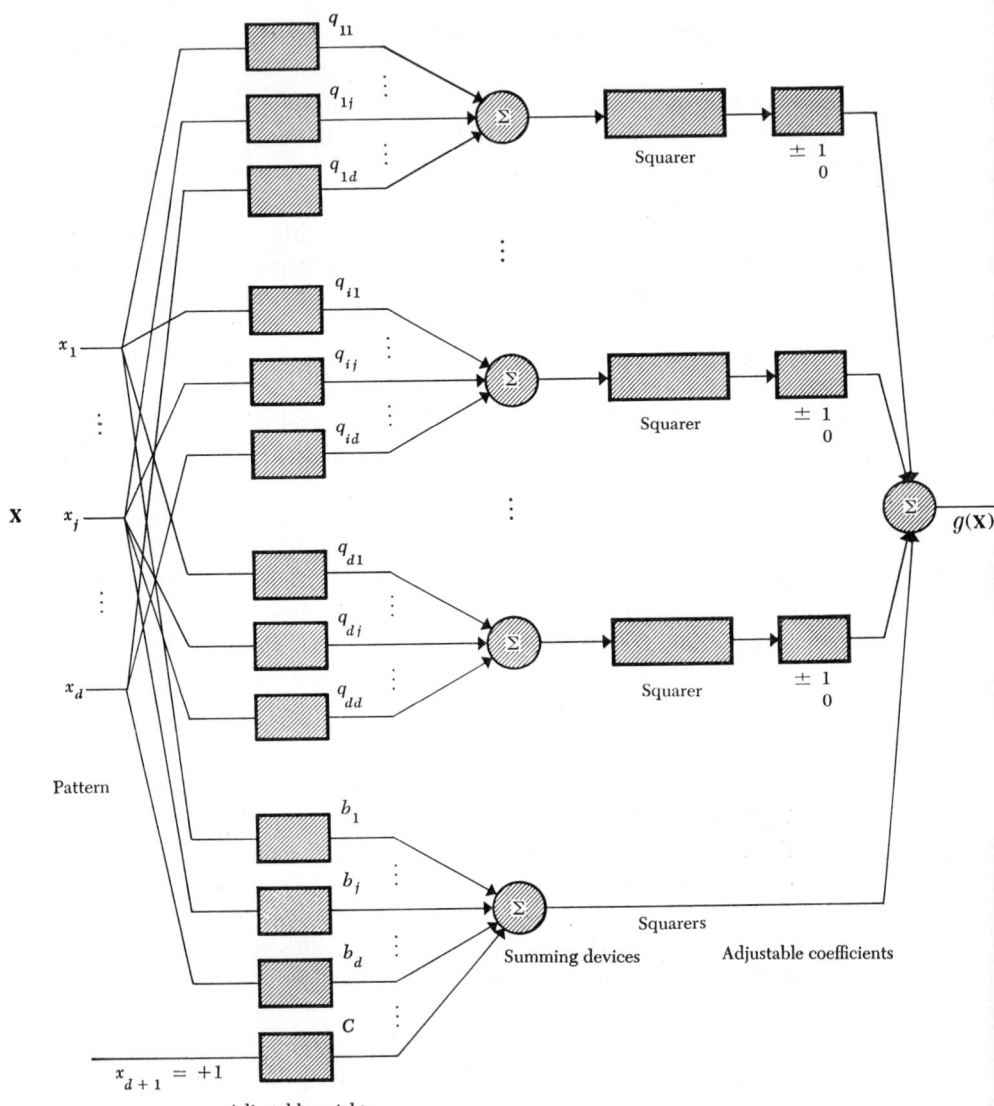

FIGURE A·1 A machine with adjustable weights and coefficients that can implement any quadric function

A·3 Transformation of normal patterns

Consider the normal distribution expressed by

$$p(\mathbf{X}) = \frac{1}{(2\pi)^{d/2}|\boldsymbol{\Sigma}|^{1/2}} \exp\{-\tfrac{1}{2}[(\mathbf{X}-\mathbf{M})^t\boldsymbol{\Sigma}^{-1}(\mathbf{X}-\mathbf{M})]\} \quad (A\cdot 10)$$

where $\boldsymbol{\Sigma}$ is the covariance matrix and $\mathbf{M}$ is the mean vector. From Eq. (A·6) we can write

$$\boldsymbol{\Sigma}^{-1} = \mathbf{TDD}^t\mathbf{T}^t \quad (A\cdot 11)$$

where $\mathbf{T}$ is a $d \times d$ matrix of the unit eigenvectors of $\boldsymbol{\Sigma}^{-1}$ and $\mathbf{DD}^t$ is a $d \times d$ diagonal matrix whose entries are the eigenvalues of $\boldsymbol{\Sigma}^{-1}$. (It is easy to show that $\mathbf{T}$ is a matrix whose columns are the unit eigenvectors of $\boldsymbol{\Sigma}$ and that $\mathbf{DD}^t$ is a matrix whose diagonal entries are the reciprocals of the eigenvalues of $\boldsymbol{\Sigma}$.)

Substitution of Eq. (A·11) in Eq. (A·10) yields

$$p(\mathbf{X}) = \frac{1}{(2\pi)^{d/2}|\boldsymbol{\Sigma}|^{1/2}} \exp\{-\tfrac{1}{2}[\mathbf{D}^t\mathbf{T}^t(\mathbf{X}-\mathbf{M})]^t[\mathbf{D}^t\mathbf{T}^t(\mathbf{X}-\mathbf{M})]\} \quad (A\cdot 12)$$

The terms appearing in the exponent of Eq. (A·12) suggest the natural transformation

$$\mathbf{Z} = \mathbf{QX} \quad (A\cdot 13)$$

where

$$\mathbf{Q} = \mathbf{D}^t\mathbf{T}^t \quad (A\cdot 14)$$

Using Eq. (A·14) we have

$$p(\mathbf{X}) = \frac{1}{(2\pi)^{d/2}|\boldsymbol{\Sigma}|^{1/2}} \exp[-\tfrac{1}{2}(\mathbf{Z}-\mathbf{QM})^t(\mathbf{Z}-\mathbf{QM})] \quad (A\cdot 15)$$

Equation (A·15) suggests that the vector $\mathbf{Z} = \mathbf{QX}$ is a normal pattern with an identity covariance matrix and mean vector equal to $\mathbf{QM}$.

From the foregoing we observe that the transformation $\mathbf{Q}$ is a transformation which takes the ellipsoidal surfaces of constant probability density of $\mathbf{X}$ into spherical surfaces of constant probability density of $\mathbf{Z}$. Therefore, $\mathbf{Q}$ converts ellipsoidal pattern clusters into spherical pattern clusters. Because the components of $\mathbf{Z}$ are uncorrelated normal variables, an implementation of the transformation $\mathbf{Q}$ (as in Fig. A·1) is sometimes called a "whitening filter." This terminology stems from random noise theory in which the samples of so-called "white" noise are statistically uncorrelated.

132   AN ALTERNATIVE IMPLEMENTATION

The spherical clustering properties achieved by $\mathbf{Q}$ are employed by Sebestyen[*] as a technique for minimizing intraclass Euclidean distances. Sebestyen seeks a nondegenerate *linear* transformation which minimizes the mean square Euclidean distance between pairs of points in a set of points. He finds that the minimizing transformation is $\mathbf{Q} = \mathbf{D}^t \mathbf{T}^t$ where $\mathbf{T}$ is a matrix of eigenvectors of the inverse of the sample covariance matrix of the patterns in the set; $\mathbf{DD}^t$ is a diagonal matrix of the corresponding eigenvalues.

[*] G. Sebestyen, "Decision-making Processes in Pattern Recognition," The Macmillan Company, New York, 1962.

INDEX

Abramson, 61, 62, 63
Absolute correction rule, 70, 81
ADALINES, 77
Adaptive decision networks, 2
Adaptive sample set construction, 125
Adjusted training set, 81
Adjustment, of discriminant functions, 8
  of weight vectors, 67, 69, 70, 75, 80, 87, 91
  of weights, 16, 66, 69, 80
Agmon, 93, 94
Anderson, 12, 13, 62, 63
Augmented pattern vector, 66

Bahadur, 12, 13, 62
Ball, 125
Banks of subsidiary discriminant functions, 26, 115
  transferring weight vectors among, 117
Basic model, for a pattern classifier, 7
  for a pattern dichotomizer, 8
Bayes' machine, 44
Bellman, 127
Blackwell, 61, 62
Block, 12, 13, 77, 78, 92, 93
Brain; 12, 13, 113
Braverman, 62, 63
Brown, 41, 42

Cameron, 40, 41, 77, 78
Capacity, of a hyperplane, 40
  of a hypersphere, 40
  of a Φ machine, 38, 39

Capacity, of a quadric surface, **40**
Center of gravity of a cluster, 53
Charnes, 92, 93
Clark, 76, 77
Classification, linear, 20
Closest-mode method, 122
Cluster point, 9, 43
Clustering transformations, 12, **131**
Clusters, ellipsoidal, 52, 131
  center of gravity of, 53
  spherical, 131
Committee machines, 97, 107
  example of training, 101
  training method for, 99
Constraints, effects of, 35
Convergence of error-correction training methods, 71, 72, 75
  of fixed-increment rule, 82, 85
  of fractional correction rule, 91
  of generalized error-correction rule, 89, 90
Convergence theorem, perceptron, 79
Convexity of decision regions, 20
Cooper, 62, 63
Correction increment, 69, 75, 80, 101
Correction rule, absolute, 70, 81
  fixed-increment, 70
  fractional, 70
Correlation, 51
Correlation detection, 18
Covariance, 51
Covariance matrix, 53, 54
  rank of, 58
Cover, 40, 41, 42

INDEX

Decision regions, 6
  convexity of, 20
  of a linear machine, 19, 20
  of a piecewise linear machine, 26, 27
Decision surfaces, 5, 18, 19
  equation of, 6, 7, 18
Decision theory, 44
Degrees of freedom, number of, for a hypersphere, 38
  for Φ functions, 30
  for a quadric function, 38
Dichotomizer, 8
  linear, 21
Dichotomy, linear, 20, 67
Discriminant, 7
Discriminant functions, 6, 15, 47
  adjustment of, 8
  families of, 15
  implementation of linear, 17, 21
  implementation of piecewise linear, 25
  implementation of quadric, 29
  for layered machines, 109
  linear, 16
  for linear machines, 10, 16, 66
  for Φ functions, 30
  piecewise linear, 24
  for piecewise linear machines, 24, 26, 96
  quadric, 27
  for quadric machines, 27
  reduction of number of, 7
  selection of, 8
  subsidiary, 24
    banks of, 26, 115
  for TLUs, 21
Discriminators, 7
Duda, 12, 13, 93, 125, 126

Efron, 41, 42, 103, 113, 114
Electrocardiograph signals, 125
Ellipsoidal clusters, 52, 131
Equation of decision surface, 6, 17, 18

Error-correction training methods, 69, 80
  for committee machines, 99
  convergence of, 71, 72, 75
  disadvantages of, 118
  graphical example of, 71
  for linear machines, 75
  numerical example of, 72
  for Φ machines, 76
  for piecewise linear machines, 116
  for TLUs, 69
Estimation of modes, 123
Euclidean distance, 16
  from a hyperplane to a point, 23
  minimization of, 131
  from a point to a point set, 24

Families of discriminant functions, 15
Farley, 76, 77, 113
Firschein, 125, 126
Fischer, 12, 13
Fischler, 125, 126
Fisher, 12, 13
Fix, 120, 125, 126
Fix and Hodges method, 120, 125
Fixed-increment rule, 70
  proof of convergence of, 82, 85
Fractional correction rule, 70, 91
  proof of convergence of, 91
Fundamental training theorem, 79

Gaussian probability-density function, bivariate, 50
  equations of, 51, 52, 53, 54
  multivariate, 54
General position, 32, 36
Generalized error-correction rule, 75, 87
  proof of convergence of, 89
Girschick, 61, 62
Green, 12, 13

Hall, 125
Harley, 12, 62, 63
Hawkins, 12

INDEX 135

Hebb, 76, 77
Highleyman, 40, 41
Hodges, 120, 125, 126
Hoff, 77, 78
Hypercube, 32
Hyperplane, 9, 19, 22
  equation of, 22
  normal form equation of, 23
  orientation of, 23
  position of, 23
  positive side of, 22
Hyperplane pattern, 67
Hypersphere decision surface, 38
  capacity of, 40

Image space, 44
Image-space cells, 105
Implementation, of linear discriminant functions, 17, 21
  of Φ functions, 31
  of piecewise linear discriminant functions, 25
  of quadric discriminant functions, 28, 29
Independent binary components, 47
ISODATA, 125
Iteration, 69

Jakowatz, 125, 126
Jones, 62
Joseph, 40, 41, 92, 93

Kailath, 62, 63
Kanal, 12, 62, 63
Kaylor, 113, 114
Keehn, 62, 63
Kesler, 77, 93
Koford, 40, 41

Layered machines, 95
  discriminant functions for, 109
Layered networks of TLUs, 95
Learning matrix, 40

Learning the covariance matrix, 62
Learning the mean vector, 58
Learning without a teacher, 125
Lewis, 12, 13
Likelihoods, 45
Linear classification, 20
Linear dichotomies, 20, 67
  number of, 32, 67
Linear dichotomizer, 21
Linear discriminant functions, 10, 16
  implementation of, 17, 21
Linear machine, 16, 17
Linear partition, 32
Linearly contained pattern sets, 82
Linearly separable subsets, 20
  pairwise, 21
List of sorting tasks, 2
Loss function, 44
  symmetrical, 46

MADALINES, 113
Mappings, 5, 30
Marill, 12, 13
Matched filtering, 18
Maximum selector, 7
Maximum-likelihood decision, 46
McCulloch, 76, 77
Mean vector of normal patterns, 53, 54
Measurements, 4
  selection of, 4
Miller, 12, 13
Minimization of Euclidean distances, 132
Minimum-distance classifiers, with respect to point sets, 24, 121
  with respect to points, 16, 57
Minsky, 62
Model, for a pattern classifier, 7
  for a pattern dichotomizer, 8
Modes, 121
  estimation of, 123
Mode-seeking training methods, 122
Motzkin, 77, 78, 93, 94
Multimodal pattern-classifying tasks, 115, 116, 121

Networks of TLUs, layered, 95
Neuron model, 76
Nilsson, 12, 13
Nonparametric decision procedures, 119
Nonparametric training, 9, 10, 119
  of committee machines, 99
  of linear machines, 65, 75
  of Φ machines, 76
  of piecewise linear machines, 116, 122
  of TLUs, 65
Nonredundant partition, 107
Normal patterns, 52, 54
  mean vector of, 53, 54
  transformation of, 131
Normal probability-density function, bivariate, 50
  equations of, 51, 52, 53, 54
  multivariate, 54
Novikoff, 92, 93
Null category, 3
Number of linear dichotomies, 32, 67

Okajima, 125, 126
Optimum classifier, for binary patterns, 48
  for normal patterns, 55
Optimum machines, 44
Overlapping probability distributions, 118
Overrelaxation, 77

Pairwise linearly separable subsets, 21
Parameters, 9, 15, 43, 44
Parametric training, 9, 10, 43, 44
  example of, 47
Partition, 106
  linear, 32
  redundant and nonredundant, 107
Pattern classifier, 2, 3, 5
  basic model of, 7
Pattern clusters, ellipsoidal, 52, 131
  spherical, 131
Pattern components, 2
Pattern dichotomizer, basic model of, 8

Pattern hyperplanes, 67
  negative side of, 67
  positive side of, 67
Pattern point, 5
Pattern, prototype, 18, 52
Pattern sets, linearly separable, 20
  linearly contained, 82
Pattern space, 5
Pattern vector, 5
  augmented, 66
Patterns, normal, 52, 54
  with independent binary components, 47
Perceptron convergence theorem, 79
Perceptrons, 2, 76, 113
Piecewise linear discriminant functions, 24, 26, 96
Piecewise linear machine, 25, 26, 115
  implementation of, 25
  training of, 116
Pitts, 76, 77
Probability-density functions, 44
Probability functions, 43
Probabilistic pattern sets, 43
Prototype pattern, 18, 52

Quadratic form, 27, 56, 127
  eigenvalues of, 27, 128
Quadric decision surfaces, 28, 38
  equation of, 28
  names of, 28
Quadric discriminant functions, 27, 127
  implementation of, 28, 29
Quadric discriminator, 29
Quadric machine, 27
  implementation of, 28, 29, 130
  weights of, 27
Quadric processor, 29

R-category training theorem, 87
rth-order polynomial functions, 30, 38
Randall, 62, 63
Rank of sample covariance matrix, 58
Rao, 12, 13
Reduced training sequence, 82

Reduced weight-vector sequence, 82
Reduction of number of discriminant functions, 7
Redundant hyperplanes, 19
Redundant partition, 107
Reject category, 3
Response, 3
Ridgway, 77, 78, 92, 93, 94, 113
Rochester, 76, 77
Rosenblatt, 76, 77, 78, 92, 93, 113

Sample statistics, 50, 57
  covariance matrix, 58
  mean, 58
Schoenberg, 77, 78, 93, 94
Sebestyen, 12, 125, 126, 132
Second-degree surfaces, 28
Selection of discriminant functions, 8
Shuey, 125, 126
Signal identification over a noisy channel, 56
Singleton, 40, 41, 92, 93, 125, 126
Solution region, 68
Solution weight vector, 67
Sorting tasks, list of, 2
Spherical pattern clusters, 131
Stark, 125, 126
Statistical decision theory, 44
Steinbuch, 40, 41
Subsidiary discriminant functions, 24
  banks of, 26, 115
Summary of book, 11
Switching function, 110
Switching theory, 40
Symmetrical loss function, 46, 47
Synaptic junctions, 76

Template matching, 18
Threshold element, 8, 21
Threshold logic unit (TLU), 21
  training methods for, 69
Trainable pattern classifier, 9

Training methods, 9, 16
  for committee machines, 99
  for linear machines, 69, 75
Training methods, mode-seeking, 122
  nonparametric, 9, 10, 119
  parametric, 9, 10, 43, 44
  for Φ machines, 65, 76
  for piecewise linear machines, 116
  for TLUs, 69
Training with normal pattern sets, 57
Training process, 9
Training sequence, 80
Training set, 9
  adjusted, 81
Training theorems, 79
  for linear machines, 79, 81, 87, 90
  for TLUs, 79, 81, 90
Transferring weight vectors, 117
Transformation of normal patterns, 131
Transformation properties of a layered machine, 103

Underrelaxation, 77
Utility of Φ functions for classifying patterns, 31

Weight adjustments, 66, 69, 80
Weight point, 66
Weight space, 66
Weight vector, 66
Weight-vector sequence, 80
Weights, 16
  of a committee machine, 98
  of a linear machine, 16
  of a piecewise linear machine, 25, 26
  of a TLU, 21
Whipple, 125, 126
White, 125, 126
Whitening filter, 131
Widrow, 77, 78, 113
Winder, 40, 41, 42, 62